T0178985

Concurrent, Real-Time and Distributed Programming in Java

FOCUS SERIES

Jean-Charles Pomerol

Concurrent, Real-Time and Distributed Programming in Java

Threads, RTSJ and RMI

Badr Benmammar

WILEY

First published 2018 in Great Britain and the United States by ISTE Ltd and John Wiley & Sons, Inc.

ISTE Ltd
27-37 St George's Road
London SW19 4EU
UK

www.iste.co.uk

John Wiley & Sons, Inc.
111 River Street
Hoboken, NJ 07030
USA

www.wiley.com

Library of Congress Control Number: 2017957888

British Library Cataloguing-in-Publication Data
A CIP record for this book is available from the British Library
ISSN 2051-2481 (Print)
ISSN 2051-249X (Online)
ISBN 978-1-78630-258-8

Contents

List of Acronyms

API	Application Programming Interface
CNI	Cygnus Native Interface
CORBA	Common Object Request Broker Architecture
DCOM	Distributed Component Object Model
DGC	Distributed Garbage Collection
FIFO	First In, First Out
GC	Garbage Collector
GCC	GNU Compiler Collection
GCJ	GNU Compiler for Java
GNU	GNU's Not Unix
IIOP	Internet Inter-ORB Protocol
IP	Internet Protocol
J2SE	Java 2 Standard Edition
J2EE	Java 2 Enterprise Edition
J2ME	Java 2 Micro Edition

JDK	Java SE Development Kit
JNI	Java Native Interface
JRMP	Java Remote Method Protocol
JSSE	Java Secure Socket Extension
JVM	Java Virtual Machine
KVM	Kilo VM
OSI	Open Systems Interconnection
PCP	Priority Ceiling Protocol
PIP	Priority Inheritance Protocol
RMI	Remote Method Invocation
RMIC	RMI Compiler
RPC	Remote Procedure Call
RRL	Remote Reference Layer
RTSJ	Real-Time Specification for Java
SSL	Secure Sockets Layer
TCP	Transmission Control Protocol
TLS	Transport Layer Security
UDP	User Datagram Protocol
URL	Uniform Resource Locator
WinCE	Windows Embedded Compact

Introduction

This book constitutes an introduction to real-time and distributed concurrent computing, using Java object-oriented language as a support tool for describing algorithms. It describes in particular the synchronization mechanisms (in cooperation and in competition) and data-sharing mechanisms (internal class, static type variables) between threads in Java. We then discuss the use of Java for real-time applications. Subsequently, a presentation of RTSJ (Real-Time Specification for Java) is also introduced in this book. Finally, a presentation of distributed computing can also be found. We focus in particular on low-level communication using TCP Sockets and high-level communication using Java RMI (Remote Method Invocation) middleware. The book also contains an appendix including a set of practical application exercises in relation to the theme of the book. Knowledge of Java language is a prerequisite to properly understanding this book.

1

Introduction to Threads in Java

1.1. Processes versus threads

The operating system is tasked with allocating the necessary resources (memory, processing time, inputs/outputs) to the processes and ensuring they do not interfere with one another (isolation) [TAN 01].

This principle is illustrated in the following example in which variable a is defined in two different classes. When executing both classes, the two allocated memory zones for this variable are completely isolated.

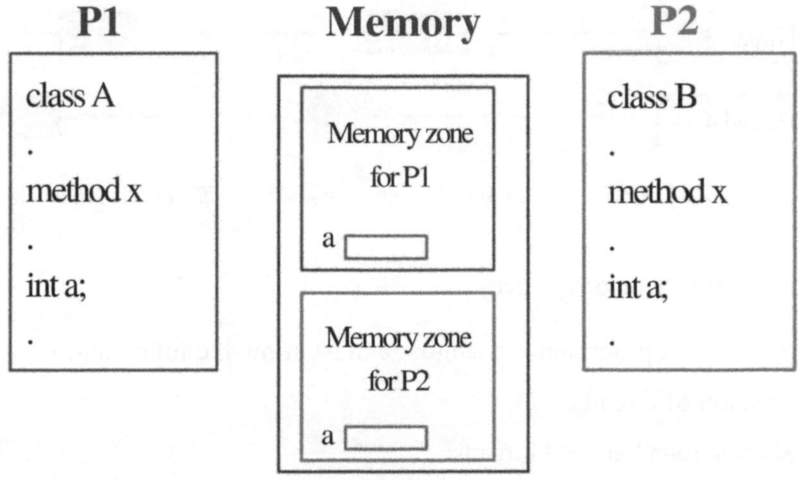

Figure 1.1. *Isolation between processes*

Most operating systems offer a distinction between:

– Heavy-weight processes: supposedly completely separate from one another.

– Light-weight processes (threads): which share a memory space (as well as other resources) in common.

DEFINITION 1.– A thread is a string of code capable of executing alongside other processes. Threads do not execute at the same time but rather using shared time, this is why it is important that a thread always gives others a chance to execute.

The diagram below shows the execution and latency times for four different threads.

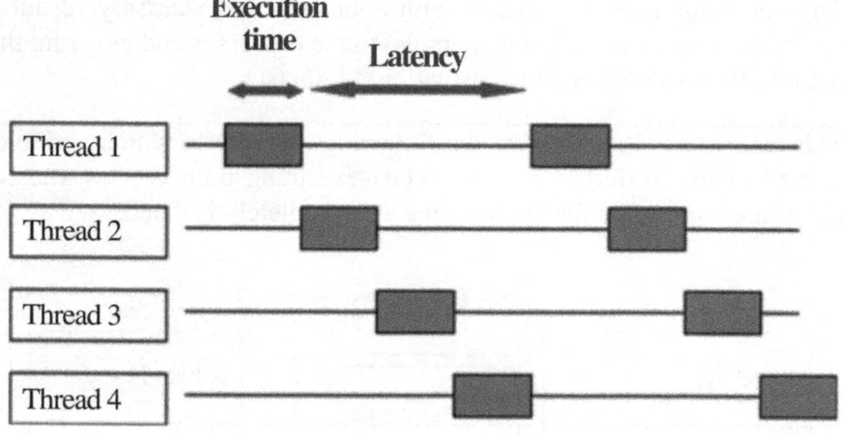

Figure 1.2. *Execution and latency times of four different threads*

1.2. Concurrent computing

A concurrent programming language must allow the following:

– creation of threads;

– sharing data between threads;

– synchronization among threads: controlling the task execution order depending on the two following models:

- Competition synchronization: when more than one thread is using the same resource. There must then be a system for mutual exclusion in order to avoid processes interfering with each other.

- Cooperation synchronization: when one thread waits for another to finish executing before starting its own execution.

1.3. Thread creation

There are two ways to create a thread in Java:

– A class derived from java.lang.Thread:

- The java.lang.Thread implements Runnable class.

- Thread extends Object implements Runnable public class.

- The Thread class must implement the run() method.

- The daughter class inherits the run() method.

– A class that implements the Runnable interface:

- The class must implement the run() method.

Now, a question arises: which solution should we choose?

– Method 1: subclassing Thread:

- When parallelizing a class which does not inherit from another class (autonomous class).

- Note: simple inheritance in java.

- extends Thread or implements Runnable, either way.

– Method 2: implement Runnable:

- When a superclass is imposed.

- Example, case involving applets:

```
public class MyThreadApplet extends Applet implements Runnable { }
```

- Only implements Runnable is valid.

Let us look at the code:

– Method 1: subclassing Thread

```
class A extends Thread {
A ( ) {...} // The constructor
...
public void run ( ) {
... // What the Thread does
}
}
A p1 = new A( ); // Creation of thread p1
p1.start(); // Starts the thread and executes p1.run()
```

– Method 2: class that implements Runnable

```
class B implements Runnable {
B ( ) { ...} // Constructor
...
public void run() {
... // What the Thread does
}
}
B p = new B( );
Thread p2 = new Thread(p);
...
p2.start(); // Starts the thread and executes p.run()
```

1.4. Types of thread

Two types of thread exist:

– User threads: this type of thread's activity is time-restricted, meaning its scenario is a process which ends after a certain amount of time. The JVM functions as long as there are user threads being executed.

– Daemon threads: threads that execute in the background as long as the program is running. Daemon threads are only there to serve user threads. The JVM stops if there are only daemons.

Examples: syntax coloring in editors, garbage collectors (DestroyJavaVM), etc.

– public final boolean isDaemon() in the Thread class to determine the thread's type.

– public final void setDaemon (boolean) of the Thread class indicates whether the thread will be a daemon or not (user thread by default).

– It must be called before the thread starts using the start() command.

– Use setDaemon in the constructor.

Example: clock thread running in the background.

```
Clock class extends Thread {
 public clock () { setDaemon (true); }
 public void run () {
  while (true) {
   try {Thread.sleep (300) ;} catch (InterruptedException e) {}
   System.out.println ("tip");
  } // end while
 }// end run
public static void main(String arg[]){
A p1 = new A( );
p1.start();
}// end main
}// end class
```

1.5. Monotask versus multitask

To illustrate multitask, let us begin by presenting a monotask execution. In the following example, a parrot (Parrot0.java) converses in monotask with the primary program (ChatAndLaunchTheParrot0.java):

```
class ChatAndLaunchTheParrot0 {
 public static void main(String args[]) {
  Parrot0 parrot = new Parrot0 ("coco",4);
```

```
    blabla(); blabla();
    parrot.run ();
    for (int n=0; n<3; n++) {
      try {Thread.sleep(1000);}
      catch (InterruptedException e) {
        System.out.println (e.getMessage ());
        System.exit(1); }
      blabla ();
    }
  }// end main
  private static void blabla() {
    System.out.println("blabla");
  }
}// end class

class Parrot0 {
  private String cri = null;
  private int fois = 0;
  public Parrot0 (String s, int i)   {
    cri = s;
    fois = i;
  }
  public void run () {
    for (int n=0; n<fois; n++)  {
      try {Thread.sleep (1000);} catch (InterruptedException e) {
      System.out.println(e.getMessage()); System.exit(1);
      }
      System.out.println (cri);
    }  // end for
  } // end run
} // end class
```

Executing the previous code results in the following:

```
blabla
blabla
```

```
coco
coco
coco
coco
blabla
blabla
blabla
```

Nothing special, the primary program talks, passes to the parrot's run and the execution ends with the three blabla of the primary program.

To perform the multitask, a modification of the previous code is necessary. We will perform this in two different ways.

– Extending the Thread class:

```
class ChatAndLaunchTheParrot2{
 public static void main(String args[]) {
Parrot2 parrot = new Parrot2 ("coco",10);
parrot.start();
   for (int n=0; n<10; n++) {
    try {
      Thread.sleep(1000);
    }
    catch(InterruptedException e) { }
    blabla();
   }
 }
 private static void blabla() {
   System.out.println("blabla");
 }
}

class Parrot2 extends Thread{
 private String cri = null;
 private int fois = 0;
```

```
    public Parrot2 (String s, int i)  {
      cri = s;
      fois = i;
    }
    public void run ( ){
      for (int n=0; n<fois; n++) {
        try {
          Thread.sleep(1000);
        }
        catch(InterruptedException e) { }
        System.out.println (cri);
      }
    }
  }
```

Executing the previous code results in the following:

```
coco
blabla
coco
blabla
coco
blabla
coco
blabla
coco
blabla
coco
blabla
coco
blabla
coco
blabla
```

```
coco
blabla
coco
blabla
```

– Implementing the Runnable interface:

```
class ChatAndLaunchTheParrot1{
 public static void main(String args[]) {
Parrot1 objectParrot = new Parrot1 ("coco",10);
   Thread ThreadParrot = new Thread (objectParrot);
   ThreadParrot.start();
   for (int n=0; n<10; n++) {
    try {
     Thread.sleep(1000);
    }
    catch(InterruptedException e) { }
    blabla();
   }
  }
  private static void blabla() {
   System.out.println("blabla");
  }
 }
class Parrot1 implements Runnable {
  private String cri = null;
  private int fois = 0;
  public Parrot1 (String s, int i)  {
   cri = s;
   fois = i;
  }
  public void run (){
   for (int n=0; n<fois; n++) {
    try {
```

```
            Thread.sleep(1000);
          }
          catch(InterruptedException e) { }
          System.out.println (cri);
        }
      }
    }
```

Executing the previous code results in the following:

```
blabla
coco
blabla
coco
blabla
coco
blabla
coco
blabla
coco
blabla
coco
blabla
coco
blabla
coco
blabla
coco
blabla
coco
```

– run() is the method to redefine in order to place the Thread's function.

– start() is a method that authorizes the Thread to initialize, and therefore the execution of run. All it does is initialize the Thread and (not blocking the calling Thread) does not wait for run to finish executing.

– It immediately returns to the execution of the calling Thread. The run method of the Thread executes at the same time as the other Threads (multitask).

– start() authorizes the Thread to start, but not necessarily immediately.

The following example simulates a race using threads. The idea is to simulate a 1000 m race between two people named Jean and Paul. Since it is necessary to have them running concurrently, each one of them will be taken on by a thread.

The following program creates a general Runner class which inherits the Thread.

```
class Runner extends Thread {
public Runner (String str) {
 super(str);
 }
public void run() {
 // Value i is incremented at the passage of the nth hundred meters
 for (int i =1; i<=10; i++) {
 System.out.println(i*100 + " m  : " + getName());
 try {
sleep((int)(Math.random() * 1000));
 } catch (InterruptedException e) {}
 } // end for
 System.out.println( getName()+ " finishes  ! ");
}// end run
} // end class
```

The test class, Race, is tasked with creating Runner instances and launching them in the race with start().

```
class Race {
  public static void main (String[] args) {
  System.out.println("Passing: ");
  Runner Jean = new Runner ("Jean");
```

```
        Runner Paul = new Runner ("Paul");
        Jean.start();
        Paul.start();
    }
   }
```

Executing this code results in the following:

```
Passing:
100 m : Jean
100 m : Paul
200 m : Jean
200 m : Paul
300 m : Paul
300 m : Jean
400 m : Jean
500 m : Jean
600 m : Jean
400 m : Paul
700 m : Jean
500 m : Paul
600 m : Paul
800 m : Jean
900 m : Jean
1000 m : Jean
700 m : Paul
Jean finishes!
800 m : Paul
900 m : Paul
1000 m : Paul
Paul finishes!
```

1.6. Different states of a thread

A thread can be in one of the four following states:

– New: includes all moments between when it is created (by a constructor) and the call for its start() method.

– Runnable: immediately after the start method is called.

– Blocked: representing the moments where the thread is waiting, for example, when it is suspended by the sleep (long) method which pauses the execution of the thread for a given amount of time.

– Terminated: when its run() method ends.

The state of a thread can be specified by the call for its getState() method.

1.7. Lifecycle of a thread

The lifecycle of a thread illustrates that it can be suspended by:

– waiting for the end of a sleep;

– waiting for an entry–exit block to end;

– waiting for a wait synchronization.

Figure 1.3 shows the lifecycle of a thread.

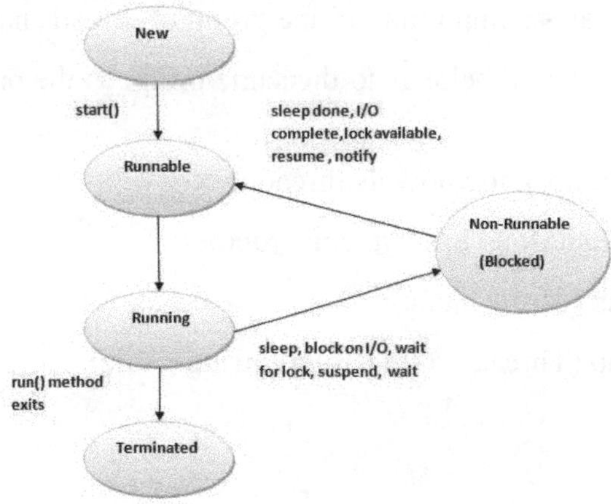

Figure 1.3. *Lifecycle of a thread*

For the creation of threads in Java, we have eight constructors (constructor surcharge) [ORA 17a]:

– Thread();

– Thread(Runnable target);

– Thread(Runnable target, String name);

– Thread(String name);

– Thread(ThreadGroup group, Runnable target);

– Thread(ThreadGroup group, Runnable target, String name);

– Thread(ThreadGroup group, Runnable target, String name, long stackSize);

– Thread(ThreadGroup group, String name).

NOTE.– Numerous threads can execute simultaneously, it would be useful to be able to control them as one single entity: to suspend them, stop them, etc.

Java offers this possibility via the use of thread groups: java.lang.ThreadGroup [ORA 17b].

– We group a named set of threads.

– They are controlled as one single unit.

– The JVM creates a minimum of one group of threads named the main.

– By default, a thread belongs to the same group as the one that created it (its parent).

– getThreadGroup(): to know its thread group.

The class ThreadGroup has two constructors:

– ThreadGroup (String name);

– ThreadGroup (ThreadGroup parent, String name).

The following code creates a group of threads containing three threads:

```
ThreadGroup groupe1 = new ThreadGroup ("GP1");
Thread p1 = new Thread (groupe1, "P1"); // 8th Thread constructor
Thread p2 = new Thread (groupe1, "P2");
Thread p3 = new Thread (groupe1, "P3");
```

Control of the ThreadGroup goes through the use of standard methods that are shared with Thread: interrupt(), destroy().

For example: applying the interrupt() method to GP1 means invoking this method for each Thread within the group (P1, P2 and P3).

The following code shows the creation of a thread tree:

```
// 1st ThreadGroup constructor
ThreadGroup groupe1 = new ThreadGroup("GP1");
Thread p1 = new Thread(groupe1, "P1");
Thread p2 = new Thread(groupe1, "P2");
Thread p3 = new Thread(groupe1, "P3");
// 2nd ThreadGroup constructor
ThreadGroup groupe11 = new ThreadGroup(groupe1, "GP11");
Thread p4 = new Thread(groupe11, "P4");
Thread p5 = new Thread(groupe11, "P5");
```

which gives us the following tree diagram:

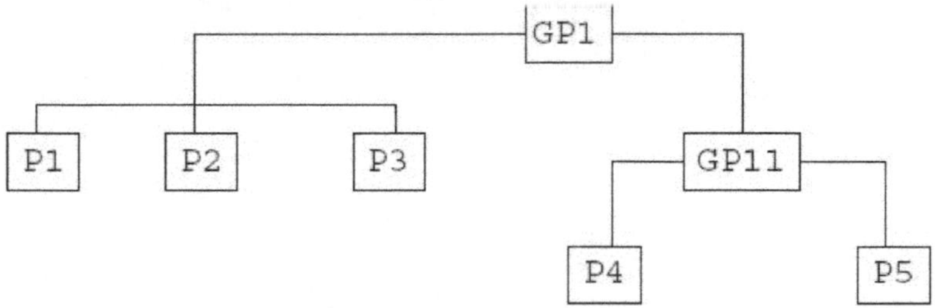

Figure 1.4. *Thread tree*

1.8. A few notes concerning threads

1.8.1. *Two threads without using sleep*

In the following segment, we will launch two threads without using sleep, the primary program and another thread.

```
class ChatAndLaunchTheParrot7 {
 public static void main(String args[]) {
  Parrot7 parrot = new Parrot7("coco",10);
   parrot.start();
   for (int n=0; n<10; n++)  blabla();
 }
 private static void blabla() {   System.out.println("blabla"); }
}
class Parrot7 extends Thread {
 private String cri = null;
 private int fois = 0;
 public Parrot7(String s, int i)  {
   cri = s;
   fois = i;
}
 public void repeter() {  System.out.println(cri);  }
 public void run() {
   for (int n=0; n<fois; n++)      repeter();
 }
}
```

Execution:

```
blabla
blabla
blabla
blabla
blabla
blabla
```

```
blabla
blabla
blabla
blabla
coco
coco
coco
coco
coco
coco
coco
coco
coco
coco
```

This is clearly a multitask execution but the execution time is too short to visualize the allocation of the CPU between the two threads.

1.8.2. *Time allocation between two threads*

In order to visualize the allocation of time between two threads, we will have to increase the number of iterations to 5 million by examining which thread executes in multiples of 500 thousand.

The code is as follows:

```
public class InfernalRace1 {
 public static void main(String[] args){
  Runner A = new Runner("A");
  Runner B = new Runner("B");
  A.start();
  B.start();
} // end main
} // end class InfernalRace1

class Runner extends Thread {
 String nom;
```

```
 public Runner(String name) {
   super(name);
   this.name = name;
 }
 public void run() {
      long PedalStroke  = 0;
      while (PedalStroke < 5000000) {
        PedalStroke++;
          if ((PedalStroke % 500000) == 0) {
System.out.println("Runner " + name + " performs " + PedalStroke + " pedal
strokes.");
          }   // end if
        } // end while
}// end run
}// end class Runner
```

Execution:

Runner A performs 500000 pedal strokes.
Runner B performs 500000 pedal strokes.
Runner B performs 1000000 pedal strokes.
Runner A performs 1000000 pedal strokes.
Runner B performs 1500000 pedal strokes.
Runner A performs 1500000 pedal strokes.
Runner A performs 2000000 pedal strokes.
Runner B performs 2000000 pedal strokes.
Runner A performs 2500000 pedal strokes.
Runner B performs 2500000 pedal strokes.
Runner A performs 3000000 pedal strokes.
Runner B performs 3000000 pedal strokes.
Runner A performs 3500000 pedal strokes.
Runner B performs 3500000 pedal strokes.
Runner A performs 4000000 pedal strokes.
Runner B performs 4000000 pedal strokes.
Runner A performs 4500000 pedal strokes.

Runner B performs 4500000 pedal strokes.
Runner A performs 5000000 pedal strokes.
Runner B performs 5000000 pedal strokes.

CONCLUSION.– Java does not require that the system be "time-sliced": that is, the same amount of time is given to threads with the same level of priority.

1.8.3. *Priority between threads*

The setPriority method sets a level of priority between the different threads. The value must be between a minimum value, MIN_PRIORITY, and a maximum one, MAX_PRIORITY.

The following code illustrates the role of the priorities between threads:

```
public class InfernalRace2 {
 public static void main(String[] args) {
  Runner A = new Runner("A"); Runner B = new Runner("B");
A.setPriority(Thread.MAX_PRIORITY);
B.setPriority(Thread.MIN_PRIORITY);
System.out.println("Thread Runner " +  A.namc  + " has priority = "
+ A.getPriority());
System.out.println("Thread Runner " + B.name  + " has priority = "
+ B.getPriority());
  A.start(); B.start();
 }
}

class Runner extends Thread {
 String name
 public Runner(String name) {
  super(name);
  this.name = name;
 }
 public void run() {
  long PedalStroke  = 0;
```

```
        while (PedalStroke < 5000000) {
         PedalStroke++;
         if ((PedalStroke % 500000) == 0) {
          System.out.println("Runner " + name + " performs " +
PedalStroke + " pedal strokes.");
         }
    }
    }
    }
```

Execution:

```
Thread Runner A has priority = 10
Thread Runner B has priority = 1
Runner A performs 500000 pedal strokes.
Runner A performs 1000000 pedal strokes.
Runner A performs 1500000 pedal strokes.
Runner A performs 2000000 pedal strokes.
Runner A performs 2500000 pedal strokes.
Runner A performs 3000000 pedal strokes.
Runner A performs 3500000 pedal strokes.
Runner A performs 4000000 pedal strokes.
Runner A performs 4500000 pedal strokes.
Runner A performs 5000000 pedal strokes.
Runner B performs 500000 pedal strokes.
Runner B performs 1000000 pedal strokes.
Runner B performs 1500000 pedal strokes.
Runner B performs 2000000 pedal strokes.
Runner B performs 2500000 pedal strokes.
Runner B performs 3000000 pedal strokes.
Runner B performs 3500000 pedal strokes.
Runner B performs 4000000 pedal strokes.
Runner B performs 4500000 pedal strokes.
Runner B performs 5000000 pedal strokes.
```

Thread A accessed the CPU first because it had maximum priority. Thread B executes at the end of thread A because it has minimum priority. Priority allowed us to define an order of execution between the two threads.

– Priority between threads: method setPriority(int).

– The priorities of threads are between 1 and 10.

– Three constants represent the limit and median values.

– The higher the value, the higher the priority of the thread to access the processor.

– MIN_PRIORITY: minimum priority (1).

– NORM_PRIORITY: normal priority (5).

– MAX_PRIORITY: maximum priority (10).

– Normal priority is assigned by default to a new thread.

1.9. Programming a task: Timer and TimerTask

In the following section, we wish to program tasks either after an initial delay (this is the case for the launch of a simulation after a certain time, for example) or after a certain delay but periodically (in the case of software upgrades).

1.9.1. *By specifying an initial delay*

The following code launches a task once after 4 seconds.

```
import java.util.Scanner;
import java.util.TimerTask;
import java.util.Timer;
class InitiateTheParrot11{
 public static void main(String args[]) {
 Parrot11 parrot = new Parrot11("coco", 3);
  Timer timer = new Timer();
  timer.schedule(parrot, 4000);
  String response="yes";
```

```
    do {
      System.out.println("blabla");
      System.out.println("blabla");
      System.out.println("would you like to continue chatting? (y/n)");
      response =new Scanner(System.in).nextLine();
    }  while (response.equals("y"));
    timer.cancel();
  }
}

import java.util.TimerTask;
class Parrot11 extends TimerTask {
  private String cri = null;
  private int fois = 0;
  public Parrot11(String s, int i)  {
    cri = s;
    fois = i;
  }
  public void repeter() {
    System.out.println(cri);
  }
  public void run() {
    for (int i = 0; i < fois; i++)  {
      repeter();
    }
  }
}
```

Execution:

```
blabla
blabla
would you like to continue chatting? (y/n)
y
blabla
```

```
blabla
would you like to continue chatting? (y/n)
coco
coco
coco
y
blabla
blabla
would you like to continue chatting? (y/n)
n
```

The definition of class TimerTask is as follows:

– public abstract class TimerTask extends Object implements Runnable.

– TimerTask is an abstract class which implements Runnable, thus a run() method; we need to inherit the TimerTask class and redefine the run() method which codes the task to be performed.

– run() is the only abstract method in TimerTask.

– A Timer starts the execution of the task.

– A Timer corresponds to a thread which will successively execute the tasks.

– schedule(task, long milliseconds) programs the task by specifying an initial delay in milliseconds.

– The cancel() method stops the Timer's programming.

1.9.2. *With an initial delay and periodicity*

```
import java.util.Scanner;
import java.util.TimerTask;
import java.util.Timer;
class InitializeTheParrot11{
  public static void main(String args[]) {
    Parrot11 parrot = new Parrot11("coco", 3);
    Timer timer = new Timer();
```

```
    timer.schedule(parrot, 3000, 2000);
    String response="yes";
    do {
      System.out.println("blabla");
      System.out.println("blabla");
  System.out.println("would you like the parrot to continue? (y/n)");
      response =new Scanner(System.in).nextLine();
    }  while (response.equals("y"));
    timer.cancel();
  }
}

import java.util.TimerTask;
class Parrot11 extends TimerTask {
  private String cri = null;
  private int fois = 0;
  public Parrot11(String s, int i)  {
    cri = s;
    fois = i;
  }
  public void repeter() {
    System.out.println(cri);
  }
  public void run() {
    for (int i = 0; i < fois; i++)  {
      repeter();
    }
  }
}
```

schedule(task, long delay, long period) programs the task after a delay for periodic executions: times are given in milliseconds.

Execution:

```
blabla
blabla
would you like the parrot to continue? (y/n)
coco
coco
coco
coco
coco
coco
ncoco coco
coco
```

The task is launched after 3 seconds for a periodic execution of 2 seconds.

2

Thread Synchronization

2.1. Synchronization upon termination: join() method

In the following example, there are two writers (EcrivainA and EcrivainB): one will write ABC 10 times and the other will write XYZ 10 times. Each word (ABC or XYZ) will be written letter by letter with a return after the last letter of each word.

The following code represents this scenario:[1]

```
public class Ecrivain extends Thread {
 private String texte;
 public Ecrivain(String t) {
  texte=t;
 }
 public void run() {
  for (int i=0; i<10; i++) {
   int j=0;
   for (;j<texte.length()-1; j++) {
    System.out.print(texte.substring(j,j+1));
    try {sleep((long)(Math.random() * 100));}
    catch (InterruptedException e) {}
   } System.out.println(texte.substring(j,j+1));
  } //end for on i
System.out.println("ecrivain de "+texte+" a fini");
 } //end run
}
```

```
public class Prog55 {
 public static void main (String argv[]) {
  Ecrivain ecrivainA, ecrivainB;
  ecrivainA = new Ecrivain ("ABC");
  ecrivainB = new Ecrivain ("XYZ");
  ecrivainA.start();
  ecrivainB.start();
 }
}
```

1 For a color version of the codes appearing in this chapter, see www.iste.co.uk/benmammar/java.zip

Execution:

AXBYC
ABZ
XC
AYZ
XBC
AYBC
AZ
XBC
AYBC
AZ
XBC
ABYZ
XC
AYBC
AZ
XBC
Ecrivain de ABC a fini
YZ
XYZ
XYZ
XYZ
Ecrivain de XYZ a fini

There is concurrence between both writers and that is the reason why we obtained the above execution. Using the join() method of the Thread class, we can synchronize the two threads. EcrivainB will be launched after the termination of EcrivainA (class Prog55.java following).

The code presented after join() will be executed after the end of the execution of the code located before join().

This type of synchronization called upon termination.

```
public class Prog55 {
 public static void main (String argv[]) {
  Ecrivain EcrivainA, EcrivainB;
  EcrivainA = new Ecrivain ("ABC");
  EcrivainB = new Ecrivain ("XYZ");
  EcrivainA.start();
  try {
   EcrivainA.join();
  }
  catch(InterruptedException e) {
   System.out.println(e.getMessage());
   System.exit(1);
  }
 EcrivainB.start();
 }
}
```

Execution:

```
ABC
ABC
ABC
ABC
ABC
ABC
ABC
ABC
ABC
ABC
Ecrivain de ABC a fini
XYZ
XYZ
XYZ
```

XYZ
XYZ
XYZ
XYZ
XYZ
XYZ
XYZ
Ecrivain de XYZ a fini

2.2. Resource in mutual exclusion: synchronized modifier

Take the following code: the print method displays a word letter by letter with a line break at the end of the last letter. The writers go through a printer to write.

Both writers are now addressing a common printer. They “squash” the text variable of the printer (*imprimeur*). The whole thing is still illegible (see the execution below).

```
public class Imprimeur1 {
 private String texte;
 public Imprimeur1() {texte=""; }
 public void imprimer(String t) {
  texte=t;
  for (int j=0;j<texte.length()-1;j++) {
   System.out.print(texte.substring(j,j+1));
   try {Thread.sleep(100);}
   catch (InterruptedException e) {};
  } // end for
System.out.println
(texte.substring(texte.length()-1,texte.length()));
 } // end imprimer
}
```

```
public class Prog56 {
 public static void main (String argv[]) {
  Ecrivain2 ecrivainA, ecrivainB;
  Imprimeur1 imprim= new Imprimeur1();
  ecrivainA = new Ecrivain2("ABC", imprim);
  ecrivainB = new Ecrivain2("XYZ", imprim);
  ecrivainA.start();
  ecrivainB.start();
 }
}
```

```
public class Ecrivain2 extends Thread {
 private String texte;
 private Imprimeur1 imprim;
 public Ecrivain2(String t, Imprimeur1 i) {
  imprim=i;
  texte=t;
 }
 public void run() {
  for (int i=0; i<10; i++) {
   imprim.imprimer(texte);
   try {sleep((long)(Math.random() * 100));
   catch (InterruptedException e) {}
  } // end for
  System.out.println("ecrivain de "+texte+" a fini");
 }//end run
}
```

Execution:

```
AXYYZ
Z
AXYYZ
Z
AXYYZ
AC
XYYZ
Z
XABBC
C
AXYYZ
Z
AXYYZ
Z
XABBC
C
XABBC
C
XABBC
Ecrivain de XYZ a fini
C
Ecrivain de ABC a fini
```

The use of “synchronized” is indispensable to resolve this problem, as is shown in the following code:

```
public class Imprimeur1 {
 private String texte;
 public Imprimeur1() {texte=""; }
 public synchronized void imprimer(String t) {
  texte=t;
  for (int j=0;j<texte.length()-1; j++) {
   System.out.print(texte.substring(j,j+1));
   try {Thread.sleep(100);}
    catch (InterruptedException e) {};
  }  // end for
System.out.println
(texte.substring(texte.length()-1,texte.length()));
 } // end imprimer
}
```

```
public class Ecrivain2 extends Thread {
 private String texte;
 private Imprimeur1 imprim;
 public Ecrivain2(String t, Imprimeur1 i) {
  imprim=i;
  texte=t;
 }
 public void run() {
  for (int i=0; i<10; i++) {
   imprim.imprimer(texte);
   try {sleep((long)(Math.random() * 100));
   catch (InterruptedException e) {}
  } // end for
  System.out.println("ecrivain de "+texte+" a fini");
 }// end run
}
```

```
public class Prog56 {
 public static void main (String argv[]) {
  Ecrivain2 ecrivainA, ecrivainB;
  Imprimeur1 imprim= new Imprimeur1();
  ecrivainA = new Ecrivain2("ABC", imprim);
  ecrivainB = new Ecrivain2("XYZ", imprim);
  ecrivainA.start();
  ecrivainB.start();
 }
}
```

"synchronized" defines a lock or a mutual exclusion on the print method: at most one thread can execute the method at one time.

This new execution results in the following:

Execution:

ABC
XYZ
ABC
XYZ
ABC
XYZ
ABC
XYZ
ABC
XYZ
ABC
XYZ

ABC

XYZ

ABC

XYZ

ABC

XYZ

ABC

XEcrivain de ABC a fini

YZ

Ecrivain de XYZ a fini

A writer, at the moment of executing the method, has this method's lock. The lock is attached to the next iteration and therefore the second writer takes over to display his text and so on until the end of the execution.

2.3. Shared variables: internal class

In the following, we will discuss variable sharing between threads. The following code illustrates a usage scenario:

```
public class PerroquetsMatheux20 {
 private int compteur;
 public static void main(String args[]) {
  new PerroquetsMatheux20();
 }
 public PerroquetsMatheux20 () {
  compteur = 1;
  Perroquet20 perroquetA
  = new Perroquet20("coco", 10);
  Perroquet20 perroquetB
  = new Perroquet20("bonjour", 10);
  perroquetA.start();
  perroquetB.start();
  try {
   perroquetA.join();
   perroquetB.join();
  }
  catch(InterruptedException e) { }
  System.out.println("compteur = "+compteur);
 }// end of constructor

class Perroquet20 extends Thread {
  private String cri = null;
  private int fois = 0;
  public Perroquet20 (String s, int i) {
   cri = s;
   fois = i;
  }
  public void repeter() {
   String repete = cri + " " + compteur;
   System.out.println(repete);
   compteur++;
 try{ Thread.sleep((int)(Math.random()*1000)); }
   catch(InterruptedException e) { }
  }// fin de repeter
  public void run() {
   for (int n=0; n<fois; n++)
    repeter();
  }//end of run
 } // end of Perroquet20 class
} // end of PerroquetsMatheux20 class
```

Class Perroquet20 is located within the class PerroquetsMatheux20, and the join method is used so as not to display the value of the counter before the termination of the two threads.

As a result of these rules of visibility in Java, the variable *compteur* (counter) is visible/accessible from the class Perroquet20 and therefore from both thread objects perroquetA and perroquetB; however, the instance variables *cri and fois* (cry and times) by Perroquet20 exist in as many copies as instances of Perroquet20. Both threads therefore access a shared/common space of variables.

Unlike processes which each possess their own clearly outlined workspace, separate from other processes.

Execution:

coco 1
bonjour 2
bonjour 3
coco 4
bonjour 5
coco 6
bonjour 7
bonjour 8
bonjour 9
coco 10
bonjour 11
coco 12
bonjour 13
coco 14
coco 15
bonjour 16
coco 17
bonjour 18
coco 19
coco 20
compteur = 21

2.4. The problem with mutual exclusions

To illustrate the problem with mutual exclusions, we will replace the counter++ instruction, located in the class Perroquet20 by its equivalent: value = counter + 1 and counter = value (*valeur*).

The two parrot (*perroquet*) threads work in alternation: one thread can be paused in the middle of executing its repeater (*repeter*) method so that the thread controller allows the other one to execute (sleep between the two new instructions in the class Perroquet21).

```
public class PerroquetsMatheux21{
  private int compteur;
  public static void main(String args[]) {
    new PerroquetsMatheux21(); }
  public PerroquetsMatheux21() {
    compteur = 0;
    Perroquet21 perroquetA
    = new Perroquet21("coco", 10);
    Perroquet21 perroquetB
    = new Perroquet21("bonjour", 10);
    perroquetA.start();
    perroquetB.start();
    try {
      perroquetA.join();
      perroquetB.join();
    }
    catch(InterruptedException e) { }
    System.out.println("compteur = "+compteur);
  }
```

```
class Perroquet21 extends Thread {
  private String cri = null;
  private int fois = 0;
  public Perroquet21(String s, int i) {
    cri = s;
    fois = i; }
  public void repeter() {
    int valeur = compteur + 1;
    String repete = cri + " " + valeur;
    System.out.println(repete);
    try { Thread.sleep((int)(Math.random()*100)); }
    catch(InterruptedException e) { }
    compteur = valeur;
    try {Thread.sleep((int)(Math.random()*100));}
    catch(InterruptedException e) { }
  }
  public void run(){
    for (int n=0; n<fois; n++)   repeter();
  }
}
}
```

Execution:

```
coco 1
bonjour 1
coco 2
coco 3
bonjour 3
coco 4
bonjour 4
coco 5
bonjour 5
coco 6
bonjour 7
coco 7
bonjour 8
coco 8
bonjour 9
coco 9
coco 10
bonjour 10
bonjour 11
bonjour 12
compteur = 12
```

The counter variable is shared, but value is different for each thread. It will happen that both threads must work on the same value before being able to increment it.

2.5. Synchronized block

In the following, the section where the arrow points is the one causing an issue:

```
public class PerroquetsMatheux21{
 private int compteur;
 public static void main(String args[]) {
  new PerroquetsMatheux21(); }
 public PerroquetsMatheux21() {
  compteur = 0;
  Perroquet21 perroquetA
  = new Perroquet21("coco", 10);
  Perroquet21 perroquetB
  = new Perroquet21("bonjour", 10);
  perroquetA.start();
  perroquetB.start();
  try {
   perroquetA.join();
   perroquetB.join();
   }
  catch(InterruptedException e) { }
  System.out.println("compteur = "+compteur);
 }
```

```
class Perroquet21 extends Thread {
 private String cri = null;
 private int fois = 0;
 public Perroquet21(String s, int i) {
  cri = s;
  fois = i;  }
 public void repeter() {
  int valeur = compteur + 1;
  String repete = cri + " " + valeur;
  System.out.println(repete);
  try { Thread.sleep((int)(Math.random()*100)); }
  catch(InterruptedException e) { }
  compteur = valeur;
  try {Thread.sleep((int)(Math.random()*100));}
  catch(InterruptedException e) { }
 }
 public void run(){
  for (int n=0; n<fois; n++)   repeter();
 }
}
}
```

Define a critical section

We must therefore find a way to define this part as a critical section. The following represents the solution to this problem:

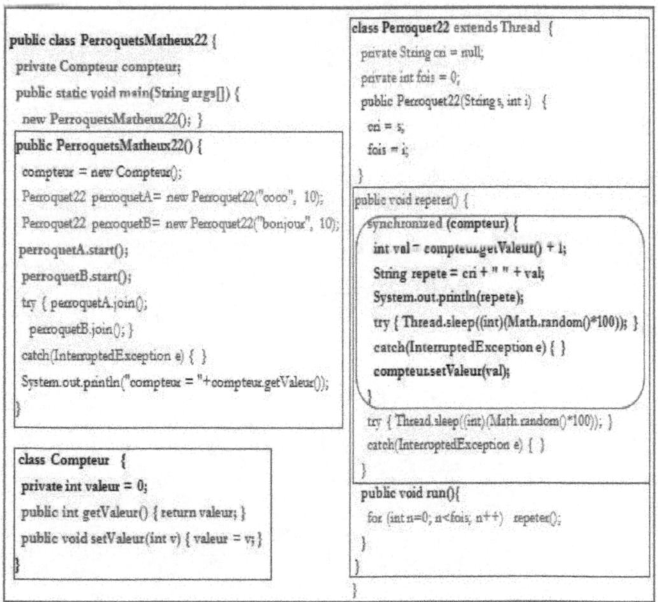

```
public class PerroquetsMatheux22 {
 private Compteur compteur;
 public static void main(String args[]) {
  new PerroquetsMatheux22(); }
 public PerroquetsMatheux22() {
  compteur = new Compteur();
  Perroquet22 perroquetA= new Perroquet22("coco", 10);
  Perroquet22 perroquetB= new Perroquet22("bonjour", 10);
  perroquetA.start();
  perroquetB.start();
  try { perroquetA.join();
   perroquetB.join(); }
  catch(InterruptedException e) { }
  System.out.println("compteur = "+compteur.getValeur());
 }

 class Compteur {
  private int valeur = 0;
  public int getValeur() { return valeur; }
  public void setValeur(int v) { valeur = v; }
 }
```

```
class Perroquet22 extends Thread {
 private String cri = null;
 private int fois = 0;
 public Perroquet22(String s, int i) {
  cri = s;
  fois = i;
 }
 public void repeter() {
  synchronized (compteur) {
   int val = compteur.getValeur() + 1;
   String repete = cri + " " + val;
   System.out.println(repete);
   try { Thread.sleep((int)(Math.random()*100)); }
   catch(InterruptedException e) { }
   compteur.setValeur(val);
  }
  try { Thread.sleep((int)(Math.random()*100)); }
  catch(InterruptedException e) { }
 }
 public void run(){
  for (int n=0; n<fois; n++)  repeter();
 }
}
}
```

– We have created a new Counter class in order to create a new “counter” object because the syntax of “synchronized” requires it.

– The keyword “synchronized” defines an instruction block which can only execute exclusively, even if other threads would like to execute it.

– When the thread perroquetA executes this synchronized block and the thread perroquetB wishes to begin execution of this same block, perroquetB must wait. Once perroquetA has finished, perroquetB can take over.

– Only one thread can execute the synchronized block at once.

– The block is said to be in mutual exclusion or even to be critical section.

– If the other threads wish to execute this section, they must wait for the critical section thread to finish.

– If there is more than one thread waiting for one synchronized block when it becomes available, the controller will only authorize one to execute.

– The sleep() call does not cause a thread to exit the critical section.

Execution:

```
bonjour 1
coco 2
bonjour 3
coco 4
bonjour 5
coco 6
coco 7
bonjour 8
coco 9
bonjour 10
bonjour 11
coco 12
coco 13
bonjour 14
```

coco 15
bonjour 16
bonjour 17
coco 18
coco 19
bonjour 20
compteur = 20

The following diagram illustrates three threads that are in mutual exclusion in relation to a single object.

The third thread will execute the critical section if it is freed by the central thread.

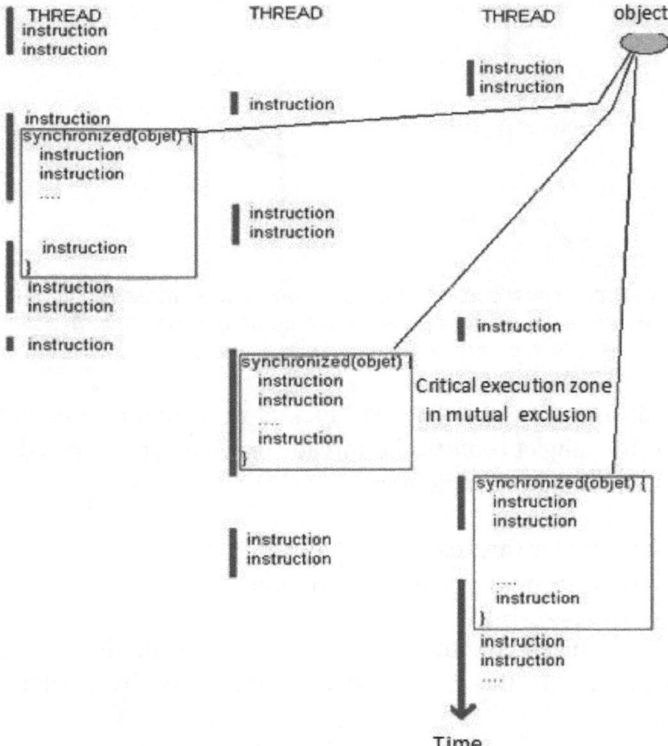

Figure 2.1. *Critical section shared between three threads. For a color version of the figure, see www.iste.co.uk/benmammar/java.zip*

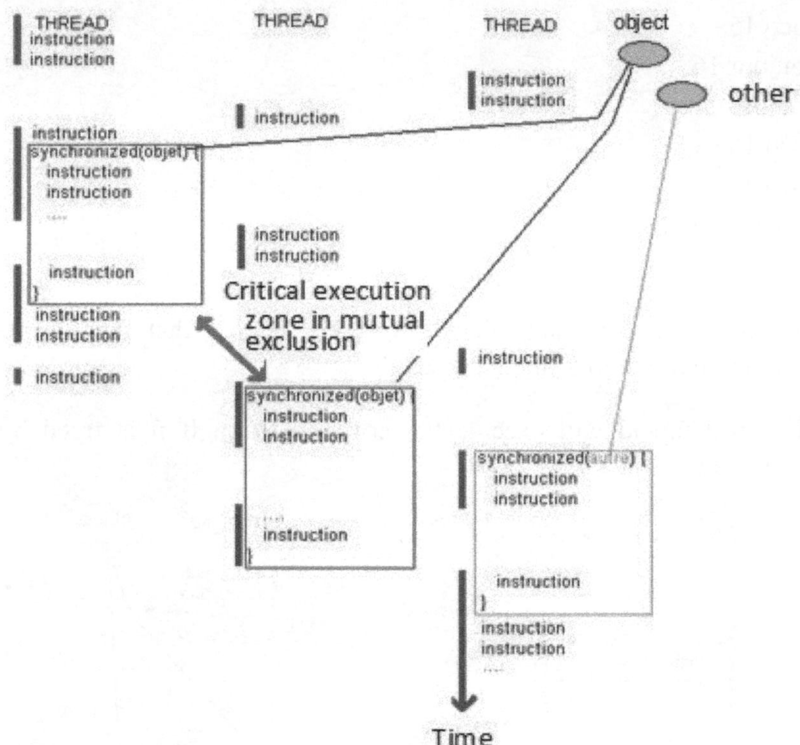

Figure 2.2. *Critical section shared between three threads. For a color version of the figure, see www.iste.co.uk/benmammar/java.zip*

synchronized(object) means that the block is in mutual exclusion relative to a *monitor* of this object (*objet*): the threads that are synchronized around the same object are in mutual exclusion.

The left and center threads have a critical section, the thread on the right has a critical section, but not with the two other threads.

The monitor "plays" the role of supervisor, ensuring that only one thread at a time can execute the critical section supervised by it: it is a locking mechanism.

The "monitor" mechanism of an object applies to all instances of Object: it is therefore a mechanism implemented within the heart of Java.

The thread that executes an object's "synchronized" becomes the owner of this object's monitor.

Thread.sleep does not remove ownership of a monitor, not even temporarily.

2.6. Synchronized instance method

In the following, we will modify the code from section 2.5 in order to create a synchronized instance method. The new code is as follows:

```
class PerroquetsMatheux23 {
 private Compteur compteur;
 public static void main(String args[]) {
  new PerroquetsMatheux23();
 }
 public PerroquetsMatheux23() {
  compteur = new Compteur();
  Perroquet23 perroquetA = new Perroquet23("coco", 10);
  Perroquet23 perroquetB = new Perroquet23("bonjour", 10);
  perroquetA.start();
  perroquetB.start();
  try {perroquetA.join(); perroquetB.join(); }
  catch(InterruptedException e) { }
  System.out.println("compteur = "+compteur.valeur);
 }
 class Compteur {
  private int valeur = 0;
  public synchronized int plus1() {
   return ++valeur;
  }
 }
 class Perroquet23 extends Thread {
  private String cri = null;
  private int fois = 0;
  public Perroquet23(String s, int i) {
   cri = s;
   fois = i; }
  public void repeter() {
   int val = compteur.plus1();
   String repete = cri + " " + val;
   System.out.println(repete);
   try {Thread.sleep((int)(Math.random()*100));}
   catch(InterruptedException e) { }
  }
  public void run() {
   for (int n=0; n<fois; n++) repeter();
  }
 }
}
```

The resulting execution is demonstrated in the diagram below.

Plus1 is a method that uses mutual exclusion and increments "val" by one unit for each thread that possesses the lock of the method.

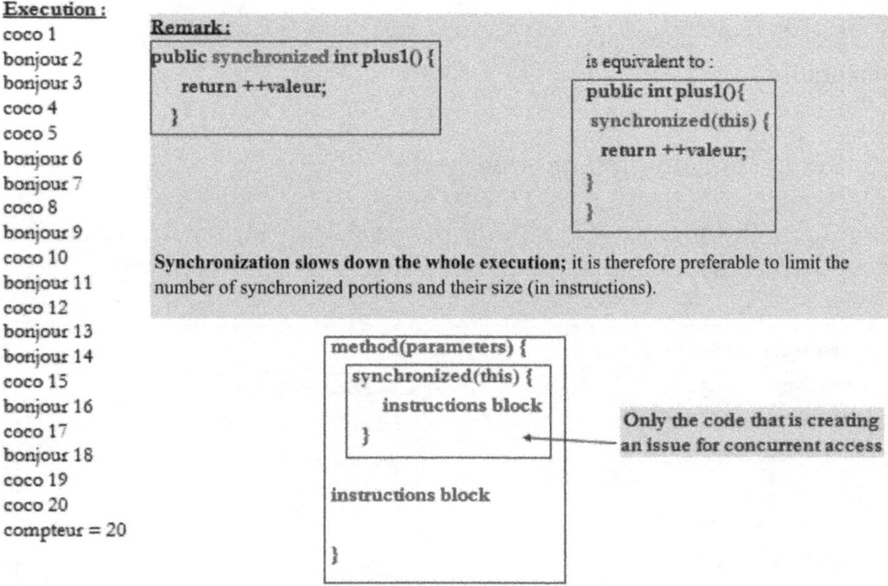

Execution :
coco 1
bonjour 2
bonjour 3
coco 4
coco 5
bonjour 6
bonjour 7
coco 8
bonjour 9
coco 10
bonjour 11
coco 12
bonjour 13
bonjour 14
coco 15
bonjour 16
coco 17
bonjour 18
coco 19
coco 20
compteur = 20
Remark:
public synchronized int plus1() {
return ++valeur;
}
is equivalent to :
public int plus1(){
synchronized(this) {
return ++valeur;
}
}
Synchronization slows down the whole execution; it is therefore preferable to limit the number of synchronized portions and their size (in instructions).
method(parameters) {
synchronized(this) {
instructions block
}
instructions block
}
Only the code that is creating an issue for concurrent access

– In Java, each object possesses a single monitor (supervisor) which can keep critical sections. It ensures that only one thread can execute the critical section supervised by the monitor,

– synchronized (object) { instr } monitor associated with the object.

– synchronized void Method(){....} monitor associated with the method.

– The object is locked while the synchronized block is executed.

– In Java, each object also possesses a waiting queue.

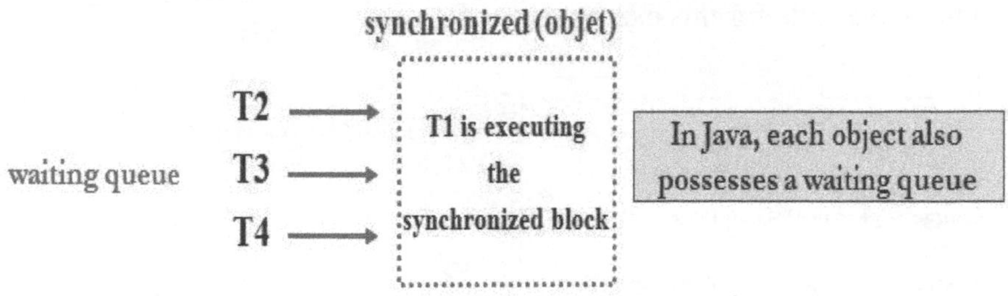

2.7. Shared variables: class variable

In the following section, we will present an example of thread cooperation (teacher vs. students). We have teacher teaching students new words.

The students must repeat each word three times, maybe more.

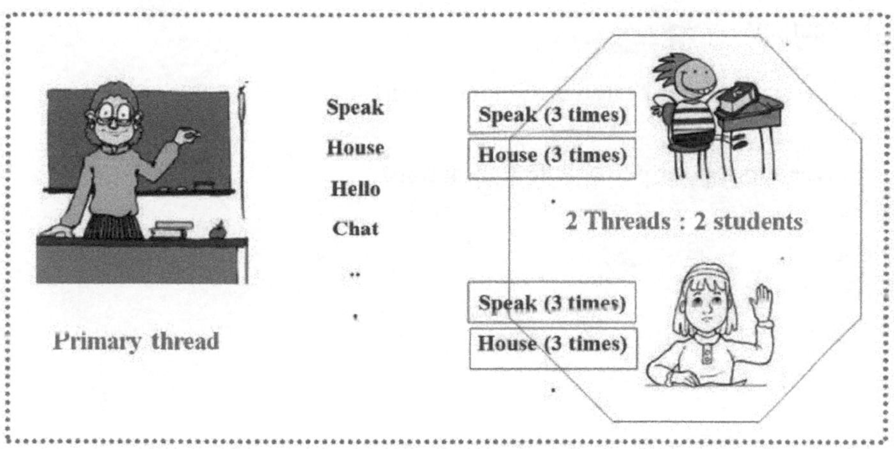

Figure 2.3. *Consumer/producer example. For a color version of the figure, see www.iste.co.uk/benmammar/java.zip*

The naive code for this example is as follows:

```
public class EcoleDesPerroquets14 {
static String mot = null;
 public static void main(String[] args) {
Perroquet14 perroquet1 = new Perroquet14("coco");
perroquet1.start();
Perroquet14 perroquet2 = new Perroquet14("jaco");
perroquet2.start();
  String reponse = null;
  do { mot = reponse;
  System.out.println
  ("nouveau mot pour perroquet ? (sinon non)");
    reponse = Saisie.litexte();
  }
  while (! reponse.equals("non"));
  System.exit(1);
 } // end main
} // end of EcoleDesPerroquets14
```

```
class Perroquet14 extends Thread {
public Perroquet14(String n)  {
   super(n);
}
 public void repeter() {
System.out.println(getName() + " "+EcoleDesPerroquets14.mot);
 }
 public void run() {
  while (true) { // tourne à l'infini
   while (EcoleDesPerroquets14.mot == null)
     try {Thread.sleep(2000);} catch (Exception e) { }
   for (int n=0; n<3; n++)     repeter();
   try{Thread.sleep((int)(Math.random()*3000)); }
   catch(InterruptedException e) { }
  }// end of while true
 }//end of run
} // end of Perroquet14
```

Execution:

nouveau mot pour perroquet ? (sinon non)
bla
nouveau mot pour perroquet? (sinon non)
coco bla
coco bla
coco bla
jaco bla
jaco bla
jaco bla
blu
nouveau mot pour perroquet ? (sinon non)
coco blu
coco blu
coco blu

blo
coco blu
coco blu
coco blu
coco blu
coco blu
coco blu
nouveau mot pour perroquet ? (sinon non)
jaco blo
jaco blo
jaco blo
jaco blo
jaco blo
.....

One static variable "mot" (known as a class variable) is shared between the two parrot threads which must learn it and then repeat it. Thereafter, the main thread enters another word (mot).

At first, they must wait with a loop for the first word and if the professor provides new words too fast, the two parrots may "skip" some!

Objective: to avoid a waiting mechanism between the professor and the parrot students: the students wait for a new word (*nouveau mot*) to learn, the professor, when teaching a word, must wait for the students to have had time to learn and repeat it, before teaching a new one.

2.8. Synchronization between threads

2.8.1. *Wait and notifyAll*

In the following code, we created an object called attheboard to share between producer and consumer. This object must have two methods: the first is used by the consumer (learn) and the second is used by the producer (teach).

```
public class EcoleDesPerroquets15 {
  public static void main(String[] args) {
    AuTableau autableau = new AuTableau();
  Perroquet15 perroquet1= new Perroquet15("coco", autableau);
    perroquet1.start();
  Perroquet15 perroquet2 = new Perroquet15("jaco", autableau);
    perroquet2.start();
    String reponse = "bonjour";
    do {autableau.enseigner(reponse);
      System.out.println("nouveau mot pour perroquet ? (sinon
      non)");
      reponse = Saisie.litexte();
    }  while (! reponse.equals("non"));
    System.exit(1);
  }// end main
}// end class

class Perroquet15 extends Thread {
  private String cri;
  private String nom;
  private AuTableau autableau;
  public Perroquet15(String n, AuTableau a)  {
    super(n);  nom = n;
    autableau = a ;
    cri = "";
  }
  public void repeter() {
    System.out.println(nom + " "+ cri); }
  public void run() {
    while (true) {
  cri=autableau.apprendre();
      for (int n=0; n<3; n++)  repeter();
    }
  }
}
```

```
class AuTableau {
  private String motAapprendre = null;
  synchronized String apprendre() {
    try { wait(); } catch (Exception e) {}
    return motAapprendre; }
  synchronized void enseigner (String mot) {
    motAapprendre = mot;
    notifyAll();
  }
}
```

Used by the students

Used by the teacher

Execution:

nouveau mot pour perroquet ? (sinon non)
master
nouveau mot pour perroquet ? (sinon non)
coco master
coco master
coco master
jaco master

jaco master
jaco master
RSD
coco RSD
coco RSD
coco RSD
jaco RSD
jaco RSD
jaco RSD
nouveau mot pour perroquet ? (sinon non)
no

– The wait and notifyAll methods are defined in the class java.lang.Object and are therefore inherited by the whole class (including notify).

– The wait method pauses (blocks) a thread's execution, until a condition is met. Meeting this condition is signaled by another thread using notify or notifyAll methods.

– When the wait method is invoked using a synchronized method, at the same time as the execution is paused, the lock set on the object through which the method was invoked is dropped. As soon as the wake condition arises, the thread waits to be able to take over the lock and continue the execution.

– Note here the primary difference between sleep and wait:

- sleep blocks the execution but the thread maintains hold of the lock (terminates its execution);

- wait blocks the execution but the thread frees the lock (a second thread can execute the critical section).

2.8.2. *Wait and notify*

In the following code, compared with the previous section, we have replaced notifyAll with notify:

```
public class EcoleDesPerroquets16 {
  public static void main(String[] args) {
    AuTableau autableau = new AuTableau();
  Perroquet16 perroquet1= new Perroquet16("coco", autableau);
    perroquet1.start();
  Perroquet16 perroquet2 = new Perroquet15("jaco", autableau);
    perroquet2.start();
    String reponse = "bonjour";
    do {autableau.enseigner(reponse);
      System.out.println("nouveau mot pour perroquet ? (sinon
       non)");
      reponse = Saisie.litexte();
    }  while (! reponse.equals("non"));
    System.exit(1);
  }
}
class Perroquet16 extends Thread {
  private String cri;
  private String nom;
  private AuTableau autableau;
  public Perroquet15(String n, AuTableau a)  {
    super(n);
    nom = n;
    autableau = a ;   cri = "";
  }
  public void repeter() {
    System.out.println(nom + " "+ cri); }
  public void run() {
    while (true) {
      cri = autableau.apprendre();
      for (int n=0;n<3;n++)  repeter();
    }
  }
}
class AuTableau {
  private String motAapprendre = null;
  synchronized String apprendre() {
    try {wait(); } catch (Exception e) {}
    return motAapprendre; }
  synchronized void enseigner (String mot) {
    motAapprendre = mot;
    notify();
  }
}
```

Execution:

coco bonjour
coco bonjour
coco bonjour

RSD
coco RSD
coco RSD
coco RSD
nouveau mot pour perroquet ? (sinon non)
encore
jaco encore
jaco encore
jaco encore
nouveau mot pour perroquet ? (sinon non)
bizarre
coco bizarre
coco bizarre
coco bizarre
nouveau mot pour perroquet ? (sinon non)
vraiment
jaco vraiment
jaco vraiment
jaco vraiment
nouveau mot pour perroquet ? (sinon non)
no

One single thread is freed from waiting by notify. Only one single parrot student is learning at a time.

notify() only wakes up one thread at a time; there is no specification on the selected thread! It is the thread controller that chooses (the mechanism is not on a FIFO basis).

A second example of producer consumer is shown in the following figure. It presents users arriving at a station to wait for a bus; a bus arrives, loads the users into the station and leaves. If one user arrives too late, they miss the bus.

```
class Station {
 public synchronized void attendreBus () {      <- Used by users (Usager class)
  try { wait(); } catch (Exception e) {}
 }
 public synchronized void chargerUsagers ()     <- Used by the bus (Bus class)
 { notifyAll () ; }
}
```

```
class Usager extends Thread {
 private String nom ;
 private Station s ;
 private int heureArrivee ;
 public Usager (String nom, Station s, int heureArrivee) {
  this.nom = nom ;
  this.s = s ;
  this.heureArrivee = heureArrivee ;
 }
 public void run () {
try { sleep (heureArrivee) ; }
catch (InterruptedException e) {}
  System.out.println (nom + " arrive a la station") ;
  s.attendreBus () ;
  System.out.println (nom + " est monte dans le bus") ;
 }
}
```

```
class Bus extends Thread {
 private Station s ;
 private int heureArrivee ;
 public Bus (Station s, int heureArrivee) {
  this.s = s ;
  this.heureArrivee = heureArrivee ;
 }
 public void run () {
  try {
   sleep (heureArrivee) ;
  }
  catch (InterruptedException e) {}
  System.out.println ("Bus arrive a la station") ;
  s.chargerUsagers () ;
  try {sleep (500) ;}catch (InterruptedException e) {}
  System.out.println ("Bus repart de la station") ;
 }
}
```

```
class BusSimple {
 public static void main (String args[]) {
  Station BusStation = new Station ();
  Bus b = new Bus (BusStation, 2000);
  Usager u [ ] = {new Usager ("A", BusStation, 1500), new Usager ("B",
BusStation, 3000),
  new Usager("C",BusStation, 1000), new Usager ("D",BusStation,
1500), new Usager
  ("E",BusStation, 1000)} ;
  b.start () ;
  for (int i = 0 ; i < u.length ; i++)
    u[ i ].start () ;
 }
}
```

The shared object is BusStation (of type Station); it contains two methods as expected. One is used by the producer (chargerUsagers) and another is used by the consumer (attendreBus).

The class BusSimple is used to launch five users as well as the bus.

Execution:

C arrive a la station
E arrive a la station
A arrive a la station
D arrive a la station
Bus arrive a la station
D est monte dans le bus
A est monte dans le bus
E est monte dans le bus
C est monte dans le bus
Bus repart de la station
B arrive a la station

2.9. Classic Producer–Consumer pattern

We will talk about classic patterns in the case of a single producer and a single consumer.

The example used here is for a professor teaching a student four new words. The student must repeat each word three times.

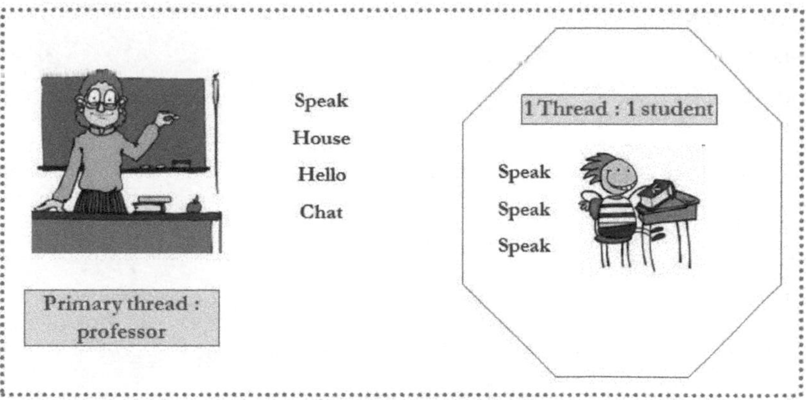

Figure 2.4. *Classic Producer–Consumer pattern. For a color version of the figure, see www.iste.co.uk/benmammar/java.zip*

The code for this example is as follows:

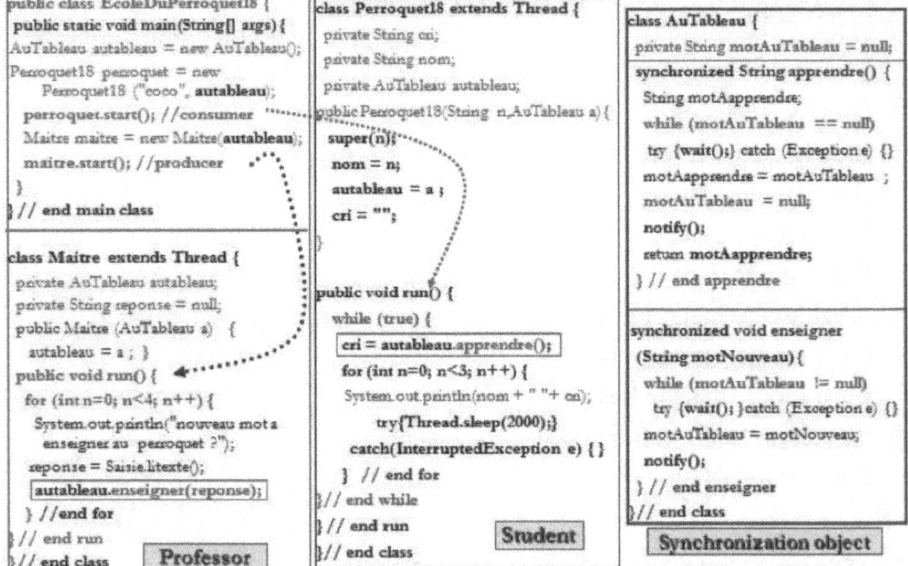

```
public class EcoleDuPerroquet18 {
 public static void main(String[] args){
AuTableau autableau = new AuTableau();
Perroquet18 perroquet = new
     Perroquet18 ("coco", autableau);
  perroquet.start(); //consumer
  Maitre maitre = new Maitre(autableau);
  maitre.start(); //producer
 }
}// end main class

class Maitre extends Thread {
  private AuTableau autableau;
  private String reponse = null;
  public Maitre (AuTableau a)   {
   autableau = a ; }
  public void run() {
   for (int n=0; n<4; n++) {
    System.out.println("nouveau mot a
     enseigner au perroquet ?");
   reponse = Saisie.litexte();
   autableau.enseigner(reponse);
  } //end for
}// end run
}// end class
```

Professor

```
class Perroquet18 extends Thread {
  private String cri;
  private String nom;
  private AuTableau autableau;
public Perroquet18(String n,AuTableau a) {
  super(n);
  nom = n;
  autableau = a ;
  cri = "";
}

public void run() {
  while (true) {
   cri = autableau.apprendre();
   for (int n=0; n<3; n++) {
   System.out.println(nom + " "+ cri);
       try{Thread.sleep(2000);}
    catch(InterruptedException e) { }
   } // end for
}// end while
}// end run
}// end class
```

Student

```
class AuTableau {
 private String motAuTableau = null;
 synchronized String apprendre() {
  String motAapprendre;
  while (motAuTableau == null)
   try {wait();} catch (Exception e) {}
  motAapprendre = motAuTableau ;
  motAuTableau = null;
  notify();
  return motAapprendre;
 } // end apprendre

synchronized void enseigner
 (String motNouveau){
  while (motAuTableau != null)
   try {wait(); }catch (Exception e) {}
  motAuTableau = motNouveau;
  notify();
 } // end enseigner
}// end class
```

Synchronization object

Execution:

nouveau mot a enseigner au perroquet?
Speak
nouveau mot a enseigner au perroquet?
coco Speak
coco Speak
coco Speak
House
nouveau mot a enseigner au perroquet?
coco House
coco House
coco House
Bonjour

nouveau mot a enseigner au perroquet?
coco Hello
coco Hello
coco Hello
Chat
coco Chat
coco Chat
coco Chat

– The problem is simplified, one single teacher and one single parrot, and one waits for the other:

- The parrot waits for a new word to learn.

- The teacher waits for the parrot to read and repeat the word.

– This classic pattern is known as Producer–Consumer:

– Both functions must be synchronized so that:

- the consumer waits until there is nothing to consume.

- while (motAuTableau == null)

- the producer waits while the consumer is not ready to consume.

- while (motAuTableau != null)

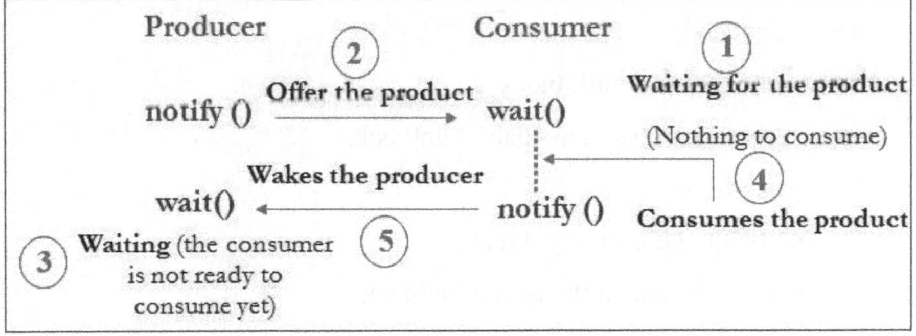

There can also be models with more than one producer and more than one consumer. One such example is as follows:

– “Producers” threads that produce data and place them into a message queue.

– “Consumers” threads that take the data from the queue.

– The producers and consumers must not access the queue at the same time (critical section).

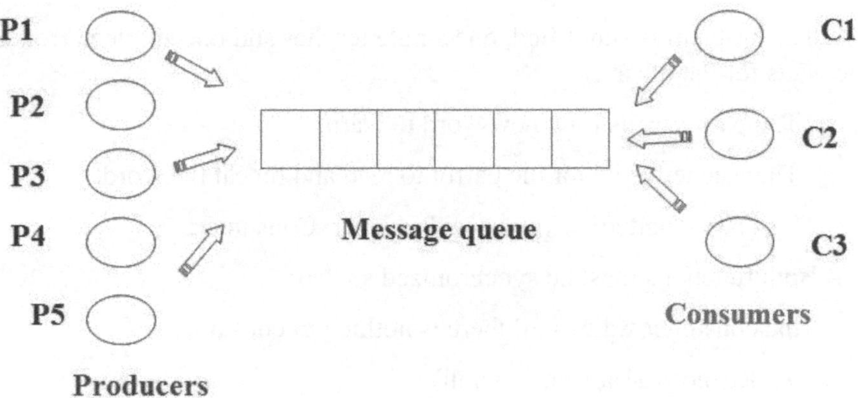

A possible implementation of this model would realize synchronization in relation to the message queue.

– The producers:

- when the queue is full: block;

- when there are spaces available: unblock.

– The consumers:

- when the queue is empty: block;

- when there is data in the queue: unblock.

2.10. Semaphore in Java

DEFINITION.– A semaphore is a high-level object that helps manage the concurrent access to a shared resource, which accepts at most N concurrent access.

Examples:

– managing entrances/exits in a parking lot with N spaces;

– managing a waiting room at a doctor's office, hairdressing salon, insurance company, etc. with N available chairs.

2.10.1. *Before Java 1.5*

A semaphore object encapsulates one whole and two atomic operations of incrementation and decrementation. The method P contains the wait and method V contains the notify.

A possible class used to implement the semaphore is as follows:

```
class Semaphore{
int counter;
Semaphore (int init)
{
counter=init;
}
public synchronized void P(){
counter--;
if (counter<0) try{wait();}
catch (InterruptedException e) {}
}
public synchronized void V(){
counter++;
if (counter<=0) notify();
}
}
```

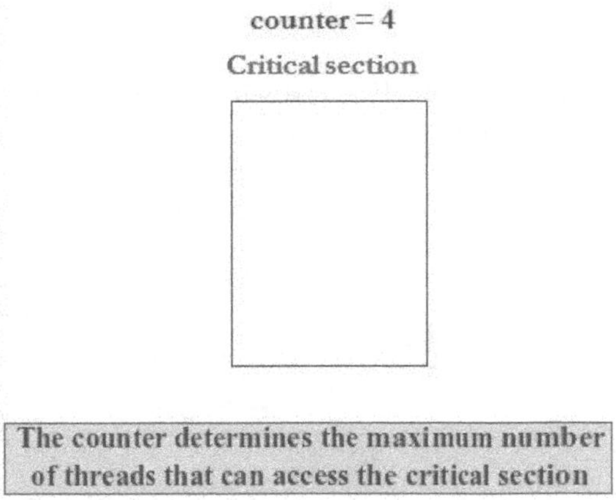

counter = 4

Critical section

The counter determines the maximum number of threads that can access the critical section

Each thread that wishes to access the critical section must use the method P and, subsequently, it will decrement the counter variable.

After access by the first four threads, the content of the critical section and the value of the counter will be as follows in the case where a fifth thread should wish to access the critical section.

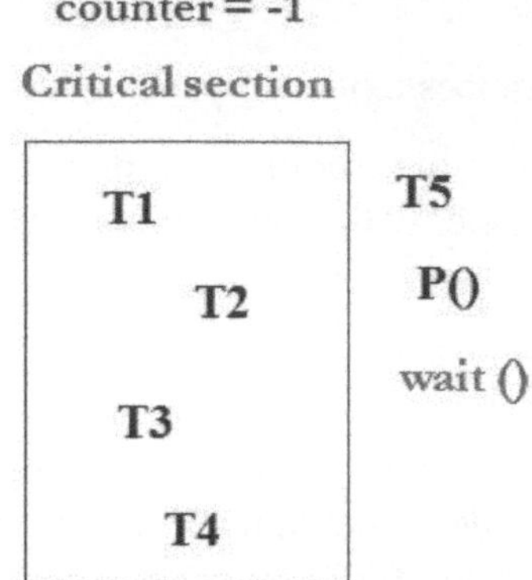

T5 is blocked because the maximum number of threads in the critical section is reached

If T4 exits the critical section, it has to use method V (increment the counter and make a notify).

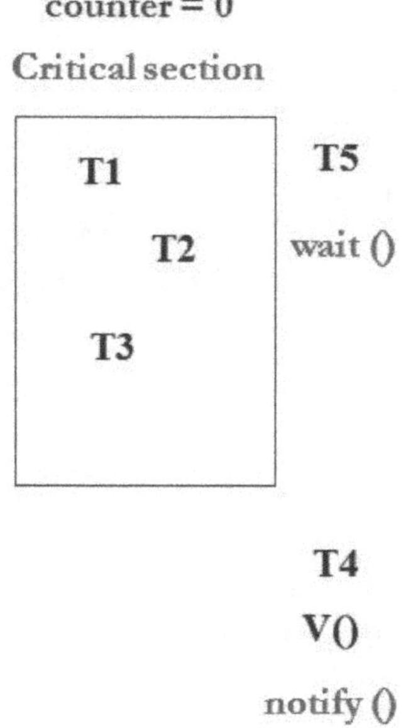

As T5 is the only thread to have been blocked by wait, it will enter the critical section after it receives a notify from T4.

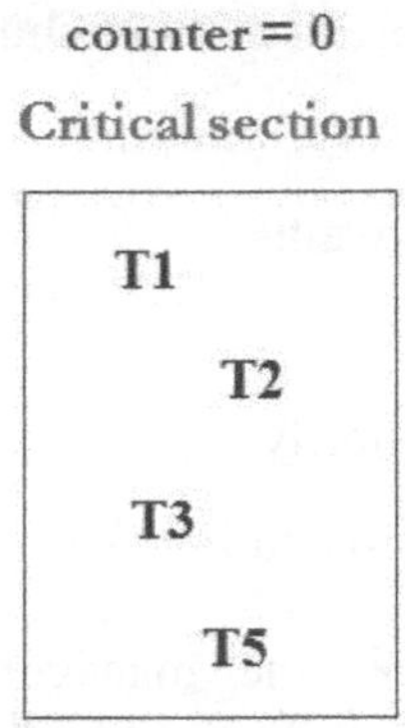

counter = 0

Critical section

T1

T2

T3

T5

After all the threads have exited the critical section, the state of the latter and the value of the counter will be as follows:

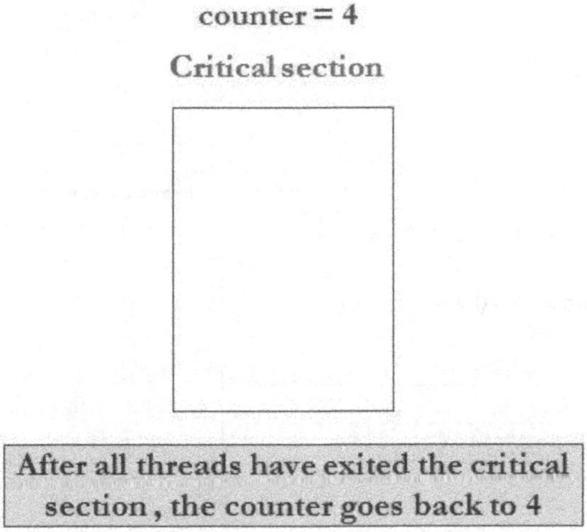

counter = 4

Critical section

After all threads have exited the critical section , the counter goes back to 4

2.10.2. *After Java 1.5*

Version 1.5 of Java and its package java.util.concurrent (along with all of its sub-packages) provide high-level synchronization tools.

– Operation P (acquire()): decrements the counter; blocks if it is negative while waiting to be able to decrement it.

– Operation V (release()): increments the counter; sends a notify if the counter is negative or null.

– We can see the semaphore as a set of chips, with two operations:

- take a chip or, if necessary, wait until there is one available;

- acquire(), usually with wait;

- put a chip back;

- release(), usually with notify.

– A semaphore has one chip and it is very similar to a lock.

The following example is the management of a parking lot using semaphores. The class parameter Semaphore indicates the size of the lot.

```
import java.util.concurrent.Semaphore;
public class Car extends Thread{
  private int id;
  private Semaphore sem;
  public Car (int i, Semaphore s) {
    id = i;
    sem = s;
  }
  private void outofLot() {
  System.out.println("Thread " + id + " is not in the
    parking lot");
    try{sleep((int)(Math.random()*1000));} catch
    (InterruptedException e){}
  }

  private void InOutParkingLot() {
   System.out.println("Thread " + id + " enters the
   parking lot");
   try{sleep((int)(Math.random()*2000));} catch
   (InterruptedException e){}
   System.out.println("Thread " + id + " exits the
   parking lot");
  }

public void run() {
      horsParking();
      try {sem.acquire();} catch (Exception e){ }
      InOutParkingLot();
      sem.release();
  }

  public static void main(String[] args) {
   Semaphore sem = new Semaphore(3);
    Car [] p = new Car[5];
    for (int i = 0; i < 5; i++)
    {
      p[i] = new Car(i, sem);
      p[i].start();
    } // end for
  } // end main
} // end Car
```

Execution:

Thread 2 is not in the parking lot
Thread 3 is not in the parking lot
Thread 4 is not in the parking lot
Thread 0 is not in the parking lot

Thread 1 is not in the parking lot
Thread 1 enters the parking lot
Thread 2 enters the parking lot
Thread 3 enters the parking lot
Thread 1 exits the parking lot
Thread 0 enters the parking lot
Thread 0 exits the parking lot
Thread 4 enters the parking lot
Thread 2 exits the parking lot
Thread 4 exits the parking lot
Thread 3 exits the parking lot

By replacing the instruction Semaphore sem = new Semaphore(3) with Semaphore sem = new Semaphore(1) in the previous code, we obtain the following execution:

Thread 2 is not in the parking lot
Thread 3 is not in the parking lot
Thread 4 is not in the parking lot
Thread 0 is not in the parking lot
Thread 1 is not in the parking lot
Thread 0 enters the parking lot
Thread 0 exits the parking lot
Thread 4 enters the parking lot
Thread 4 exits the parking lot
Thread 1 enters the parking lot
Thread 1 exits the parking lot
Thread 3 enters the parking lot
Thread 3 exits the parking lot
Thread 2 enters the parking lot
Thread 2 exits the parking lot

3

Real-Time Systems and Real-Time Java

3.1. Real-time systems

3.1.1. *Definition*

Real-time systems are different from other systems by virtue of the fact that they take into account time-relating restrictions in cases where respecting time delays is as important as the accuracy of the result; in other words, the system must not only deliver exact results, it must deliver them within the imparted time-limits.

In real-time computing, the correct behavior of a system depends not only on the logical processing results, but also on the time at which the results are produced [STA 88].

Examples:

– An ATM cannot take 5 minutes to deliver money.

– A radar cannot take 2 seconds to react.

– An ABS system cannot take more than 150 ms to acquire information and 1 second to react (ABS refers to assisted braking systems using in motor vehicles, which prevent the wheels from locking up under intense braking).

3.1.2. *Examples of real-time operating systems*

– Windows CE (Windows Embedded Compact), often referred to as WinCE, is a variation of Windows for onboard systems and other minimalist systems used, for instance, in handheld computers.

– LynxOS is a real-time operating system based on the UNIX platform developed by the company LynuxWorks for onboard applications.

– LynxOS is mostly used for onboard systems such as critical aviation software, the military, industrial manufacturing and in the communication industry.

3.1.3. *Types of real-time*

– *Flexible real-time:*

- The response by the system after a certain delay progressively reduces its use.

- Penalties are not catastrophic.

- These systems accept variations in data processing of the order of a half-second (or 500 ms) or even a second.

Examples: multimedia systems, if a couple of pictures are not displayed, it does not jeopardize the operation of the whole system.

– *Firm real-time:*

- Response from the system within acceptable delays is essential.

- The result is of no use after the deadline.

Examples: financial trading, etc.

– *Hard real-time:*

- Response from the system within delays is vital.

- A lack of response is catastrophic.

Examples: air traffic control, nuclear reactor control, etc.

3.1.4. *Architecture*

– *Monotask architecture*

- A real-time system with a single task is easy to define. All it takes is to indefinitely repeat the following list of tasks:

- Wait for stimulus.

- Act accordingly to stimulus.

Example: automatic radar.

– *Multitask architecture:*

- Each task could be performed by a thread. A resource could be protected by a critical section. The length of critical sections affects the response time from the system.

Example: intrusion detection system (IDS) that performs various tasks in real-time, including:

– Internet traffic analysis;

– identifying IPs involved in an attack;

– firewall reconfiguration;

– visual notification of the alert: displaying the alert in one or more management consoles.

3.1.5. *Task ordinance with priorities*

Priorities help organize tasks. The higher the value of a priority, the higher the priority for a task to access the processor. Priorities can be dynamic or static.

In a real-time system, a task is generally never blocked by a lower priority task.

– Consider two threads T1 and T2.

– T1 has a high priority (ex: 10), T2 has a low priority (ex: 1).

– Upon launching the two threads, T1 must execute before T2.

– At a certain point, T1 is blocked (ex: by wait()), T2 runs and enters the critical section.

– T1 unblocks and attempts to acquire the lock.

– T2 is never ordinanced and never releases the lock

– T2 executes before T1.

– Non-management of priority inversion can have disastrous effects.

– Indeed, as the absence of management of priority inversion implies that a high-priority task cannot execute, it is possible for a reaction to emergency situations not to be performed.

Example: an emergency stop order for a nuclear reactor that would be blocked by a minor-priority order.

– There is no simple solution that avoids inversions of priority. It is, nonetheless, possible to implement measures that limit these risks. In particular, it is possible to authorize access to critical sections only to similar-priority threads.

Two solutions are proposed:

– *Priority ceiling*:

- Priority Ceiling Protocol (PCP): this consists of associating a priority cap each resource. The priority of the resource among the tasks that can use it plus 1. Ordinance transfers this priority to each task which accesses this resource. When a task has finished using the resource, its priority returns to its original value.

– *Priority inheritance*:

- Priority Inheritance Protocol (PIP): when a task T2 (high-priority) is blocked while accessing resource R, the blocking task T1 (low-priority) inherits the priority of T2. T1 uses the priority inherited until the liberation of R, where it reencounters the priority it had prior to its acquisition.

3.2. Java in real-time

Originally, Java was designed for onboard devices. But Java quickly started being used for Web applications (applets). Java was then used for the following applications:

– Classic J2SE (Java 2 Standard Edition) for the client work station (JVM classic, HotSpot).

– Business J2EE (Java 2 Enterprise Edition) for the development of business applications (HotSpot).

– Reduced J2ME (Java 2 Micro Edition) for mobile systems such as personal assistant pads and mobile phones (classic JVM, Kilo VM (KVM), Card VM (JVM onboard on printed chip)).

Note that the language here is not designed for real-time, for the following reasons:

– lack of expertise in ordinancing;

– Windows has trouble managing priorities between threads;

– for notify() or notifyAll() there are no specifications on the selected thread, not necessarily FIFO;

– it is one of the few Java functionalities that is not mobile;

problems with Garbage Collector/GC;

– GC can be executed at any time;

– GC can last a given amount of time;

– GC cannot be pre-empted;

– GC pre-empts any thread.

3.2.1. *RTSJ (Real-Time Specification for Java)*

This is a proposition for extending the JVM with real-time functionalities (JVM RTSJ) [JAV 17a].

Specifications performed by a group of experts from a number of firms (Sun, IBM, QNX, Nortel, etc.).

Restrictions:

– Compatibility with existing: any non-real-time Java application can run on a JVM RTSJ.

– No syntaxic expansion.

– No material or power prerequisite.

– Predictable execution time.

– Granularity: nanoseconds. 64 bits (ms) + 32 bits (ns).

– RTSJ improves Java real-time programming in the following fields:

– Memory management.

– Clock and time-management.

– Ordinance and "schedulable" objects.

– Real-time threads.

– Management on asynchronous events and timers.

– Synchronization and resource-sharing.

– Addedpackage: javax.realtime [JAV 17b].

– Three interfaces.

– 47 classes.

– 15 exceptions.

– Four errors.

– RTSJ: Threads

– One interface:

– Schedulable: object that can be ordinanced, extends java.lang.Runnable.

– public interface Schedulable extends java.lang.Runnable.

– Two new classes:

– *RealtimeThread.*

– public class RealtimeThread extends java.lang.Thread implements Schedulable.

– Can access the heap. Of lower priority than the GC (DestroyJavaVM).

– *NoHeapRealtimeThread.*

– public class NoHeapRealtimeThread extends RealtimeThread.

– Its priority is higher than the GC. Works within the Scoped Memory, the objects within this thread are allocated to this memory.

– ScopedMemory presents the following characteristics:

– Has the lifespan of the real-time thread occupying it.

– Is not managed by the garbage collector.

– Objects can be allocated within a ScopedMemory (rather than in HeapMemory).

– Objects are free at the end of the scope.

– A NoHeapRealtimeThread cannot access the Heap.

– Therefore, a NoHeapRealtimeThread cannot be blocked by the Garbage Collector.

– Priorities are organized as follows:

– Thread < RealtimeThread < Garbage Collector < NoHeapRealtime Thread.

3.2.2. *Implementations*

The following three studied implementations are:

– *Reference implementation: RI.*

- Destined for research and aiming to demonstrate the feasibility of the Java real-time adventure. Performed by the company TimeSys [TIM 17]. It also exists for Linux/x86.

The execution of its code is presented in the following diagram:[1]

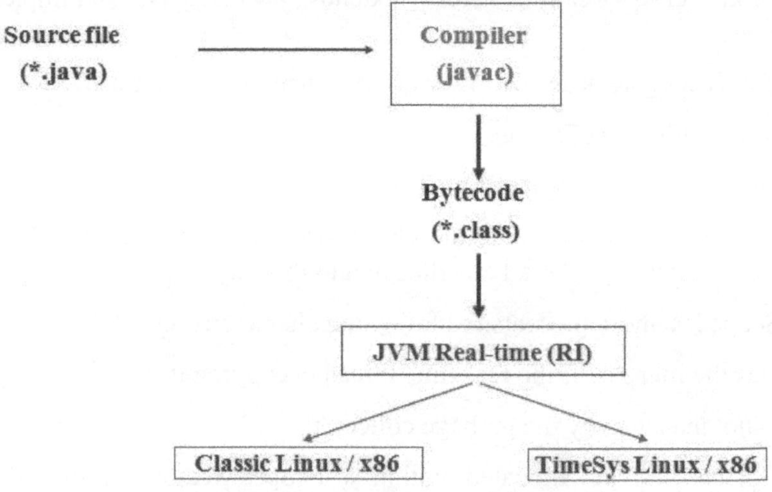

Figure 3.1. *Reference implementation*

– *OpenSource implementation: jRate.*

jRate is a university project (Irvine University in California) run by Angelo Corsaro [UCI 17].

jRate is composed of:

– Java.

– C++ (via CNI).

– CNI: Cygnus Native Interface

– The same goal as JNI (Java Native Interface): to allow access to the JVM via a language other than Java.

– CNI: only C++.

– Direct correspondence between Java and C++.

1 For a color version of the codes appearing in this chapter, see www.iste.co.uk/benmammar/java.zip

– Simpler.

– Faster.

– jRate is an extension of GCJ.

Reminder: the GNU project was launched by Richard Stallman in 1984, while he was working at MIT (Massachusetts Institute of Technology) in the artificial intelligence laboratory, in order to create a free and complete operating system. GNU Compiler Collection, abbreviated to GCC, is a set of compilers created by the GNU project. GCC is a free software capable of compiling various languages including C, C++, Objective-C, Java (GCJ), Ada and Fortran.

– *Proprietary implementation: JamaicaVM.*

This is a commercialized solution by the company AICAS [AIC 17]. AICAS is a major supplier of Java Virtual Machine, JamaicaVM, for onboard electronics requiring Hard Real-time. Aicas is present in aerospace, automotive and industrial robotics market segments. It possesses a real-time GC.

The following diagram gives an idea of its implementation:

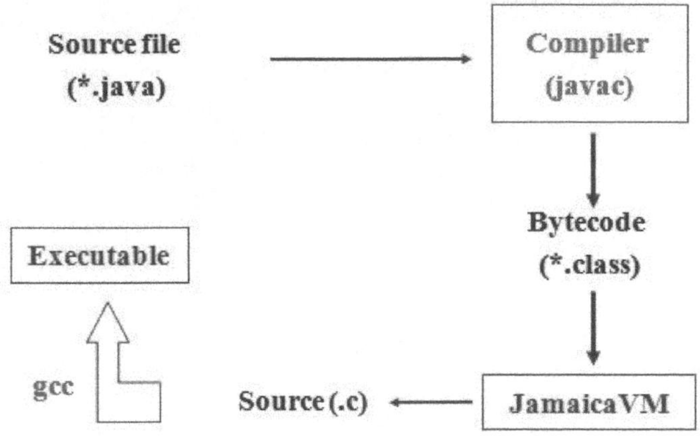

Figure 3.2. *Implementation of JamaicaVM*

4

Distributed Programming in Java

4.1. Definition of a distributed application

An application is divided into a number of units.

– Each unit is placed on a different machine.

– Each unit can execute on a different system.

– Each unit can be programed in a different language.

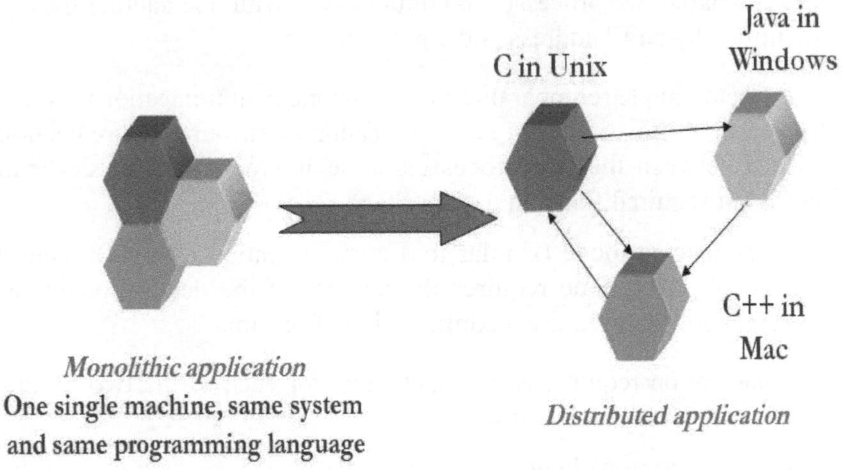

Figure 4.1. *Monolithic application versus distributed application. For a color version of the figure, see www.iste.co.uk/benmammar/java.zip*

4.2. Communication in a distributed application

4.2.1. *Low-level communication: socket*

4.2.1.1. *Definition*

A network socket is a model that allows processes to communicate and synchronize with one another, either on the same machine or over a network.

Sockets were developed by Berkeley University (California) in 1986.

The original interface designed by Berkeley was for C but since then sockets have been implemented in various languages.

For Java, the Socket class in the package java.net appearing in J2SE 1.4 (6 Feb 2002) is used to implement sockets.

4.2.1.2. *Modes of communication*

Sockets directly use the services of the transport layer in the OSI model (UDP or TCP protocols), which in turn use the services of the network layer (IP protocol).

Sockets enable two processes to communicate with one another through a link identified by an IP address and a port number.

– Connected mode (comparable to a telephone communication), using the TCP protocol. In this mode of communication, a sustainable connection is established between the two processes, in such a way that the destination address is not required for each data package.

– Non-connected mode (similar to a communication by mail), using the UDP protocol. This mode requires the address of the destination for each package, and does not require a confirmation of receipt.

Communication requires two sockets: one for each of the two programs communicating over the network.

– One socket for the client.

– One socket for the server (there is a second socket for the connection on the server side).

The mode of IP communication used, UDP or TCP, corresponds to the type of socket.

In the following section, we will focus on TCP sockets.

In Java, each instance of the Socket class is associated with an object of the InputStream class (to read the socket) and an object from the OutputStream class (to write the socket).

– The server will use two types of sockets.

– The first, called the connection socket, serves to wait for a client.

– In Java, creating a connection socket can be done by simply instancing the object of the ServerSocket class from the package java.net.

Example: ServerSocket conn = new ServerSocket(10080).

– The second, called the communication socket, is used to dialogue with the client.

– Once the connection socket is created, we will then ask it to wait for a client and obtain the communication socket that will allow it to dialogue with the client.

– Socket comm = conn.accept().

– We can then communicate with the client using the input and output streams associated with the socket.

- ServerSocket (numberPort): creates a ServerSocket object on this port number.

- accept(): waits for a connection from a slow client machine. Upon the arrival of a connection demand from a client machine, a socket is created to connect to the server. This will be the object returned with the blocking method accept().

- ServerSocket (numberPort, int backlog): creates a ServerSocket object on this port number with a queue for the connection of a size specified by the backlog.

– Connection demands, when the queue is full, are rejected and cause an exception from the client's side. By default, the size is 50.

A few methods:

– accept(): waits for a connection from a client machine.

– close(): closes the ServerSocket and any ongoing sockets obtained by its accept method.

– isClosed(): indicates whether the socket is closed.

– getLocalPort(): returns the local port number.

– InetAddress getInetAddress(): returns the server address. InetAddress represents an IP address and potentially the name of the machine.

– getHostName(): returns the host name memorized in the InetAddress type object, under the form of a chain of characters.

– getHostAddress(): returns the IP address memorized in the InetAddress type object, under the form of a chain of characters.

– getByName (String host): returns the IP (InetAddress object) depending on the name in the parameters.

The aim of the following code is to find the IP address corresponding to a machine name passed as an argument:

```
import java.net.*;
public class ResolveName{
 public static void main(String[ ] args){
InetAddress adresse;
try{
adresse=InetAddress.getByName("localhost");
System.out.println(adresse.getHostAddress());
adresse=InetAddress.getByName("www.facebook.com");
System.out.println(adresse.getHostAddress());
System.out.println(adresse);
}catch(UnknownHostException e) { }
}
}
```

Execution:

127.0.0.1
31.13.75.36
www.facebook.com/31.13.75.36

Unlike the server, the client only uses one single socket: the communication socket.

– Connection to the server and obtaining the communication socket.

– Socket comm = new Socket ("localhost", 10080).

– The Socket constructor is a blocking method on the client side.

We can then communicate with the server using the input and output streams associated with the socket.

– Nine constructors of which two are said to be deprecated, so seven constructors, including:

- Socket (String host, int port).

- Socket (InetAddress address, int port).

- Uses the IP: InetAdress.

A few methods:

– close(): properly closes the socket and is likely to raise an exception UnknownHostException.

– getOutputStream(): returns an OutputStream for the socket.

– getInputStream(): returns an InputStream for the socket.

– getPort(): returns the distant port number to which the socket is connected.

– InetAddress getInetAddress(): returns the address of the distant machine.

– isClosed(): indicates whether the socket is closed.

– isConnected(): returns the state of the socket connection.

– connect (SocketAddress adresseSocket): connects the server to the socket.

– connect (SocketAddress adresseSocket, int timeout): connects the socket to the server with an epiration value in the order of the milliseconds.

– Raises a SocketTimeoutException if the delay has already expired.

– SocketAddress is an abstract class.

– InetSocketAddress inherits SocketAddress and is a class representing an InetAddress and a port.

– InetSocketAddress(InetAddress ina, int port).

– InetSocketAddress(String hostName, int port).

– getAddress().

– getHostname().

– getPort().

The following code is used to create a socket with a timeout by using connect:

```
Socket sock = null;
try {
 int port = XYZ;
 int timeOut = 3000;
 SocketAddress sockAddr = new InetSocketAddress("host", port);
 sock = new Socket(); // The Socket constructor creates a socket with no connection.
 sock.connect(sockAddr, timeOut); // The delay is in milliseconds so 3 seconds.
} catch (UnknownHostException e) {
} catch (SocketTimeoutException e) {
} catch (IOException e) {
}
```

A connection request blocks until the connection is established or the timeout expires; if the delay has expired, a SocketTimeoutException is raised.

4.2.1.3. *Example of communication*

In the following, we present a very simple example of communication with the TCP sockets:

– The client sends a message to the server.

– The server confirms receipt and requests the next word.

– To disconnect, the client sends the word “no”.

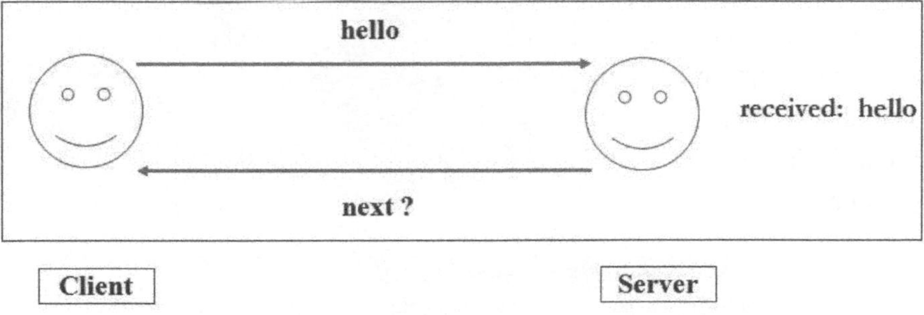

Figure 4.2. *Example of communication with Sockets. For a color version of the figure, see www.iste.co.uk/benmammar/java.zip*

The server code is as follows:

```
import java.net.*;
import java.io.*;
class ServerEcho {
  public static void main(String args[]) {
  ServerSocket server = null;
  try {
   server = new ServerSocket(7777); // connection socket
   while (true) {
    Socket sock = server.accept(); // waiting
    System.out.println("connected");
    PrintWriter sockOut = new PrintWriter(sock.getOutputStream(), true);
    BufferedReader sockIn = new BufferedReader(new
    InputStreamReader(sock.getInputStream()));
    String recu;
```

```
      while ((recu = sockIn.readLine()) != null) {
        System.out.println("recu:"+recu);
        sockOut.println("next? ");
      } //end while
      sockOut.close();
      sock.close();
    } //end while (true)
 } catch (IOException e) {
try {server.close();}
catch (IOException e2) {}
} // end first catch
}// end main
 } // end class
```

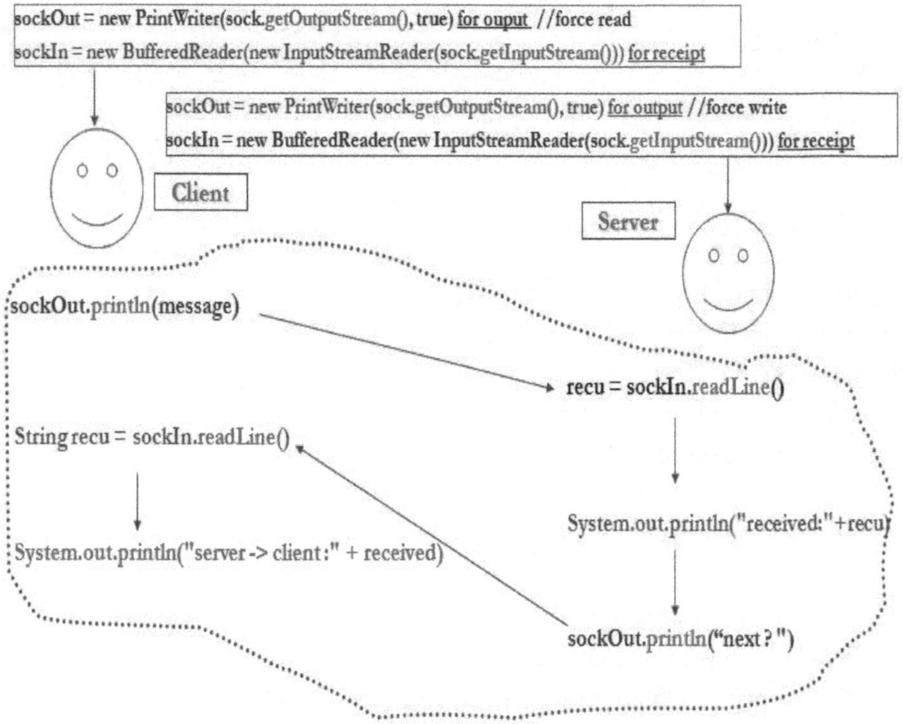

Figure 4.3. *Diagram of communication with Sockets. For a color version of the figure, see www.iste.co.uk/benmammar/java.zip*

The client code is as follows:

```
import java.io.*;
import java.net.*;
import java.util.Scanner;
public class ClientEcho {
 public static void main(String[] args) throws IOException {
  Socket sock = null;
  PrintWriter sockOut = null;
  BufferedReader sockIn = null;
  try {sock = new Socket("localhost", 7777); // the communication socket.
   sockOut = new PrintWriter(sock.getOutputStream(), true); //force write
   sockIn = new BufferedReader(new InputStreamReader(sock.getInput
Stream()));
  } catch (UnknownHostException e) {
   System.err.println("host unreachable: localhost");
   System.exit(1);
  } catch (IOException e) {
   System.err.println("cannot connect to: localhost");
   System.exit(1);
  }
  System.out.println("press any key to close");
  Scanner scan = new Scanner(System.in);
  String message = scan.next().toLowerCase();
  while (! message.equals("no")) {
   sockOut.println(message);
   String recu = sockIn.readLine();
   System.out.println("server -> client:" + recu);
   message = scan.next().toLowerCase();
  }
  sockOut.close();
  sockIn.close();
  sock.close();
 }
}
```

The execution is as follows:

– On the server side:

```
connected
received: hello
received: bye
```

– Client side:

```
press any key to close
hello
server -> client: next ?
bye
server -> client: next ?
no
```

Note that, for the characters, the Java language uses the "char" type based on Unicode encoded in 16 bit. The transmission over the networks is based on an 8 bit byte.

Telecommunication methods for Java are therefore based on the transfer of bytes.

– Convert a String into bytes[ ]:

- String chaine = "ABCD";

- byte[ ] message=chaine.getBytes();

– Convert a byte[ ] into a String:

- chaine = new String(message);

4.2.1.4. *Direct write onto the stream of a socket*

The following code enables direct writing onto the stream of a socket:

```
OutputStream sockOut = socket.getOutputStream();
// Obtain the writing OutputStream of the socket.
// We use it directly to write new bytes.
byte[ ] buffer = new byte[1024];
```

```
buffer = "ABCD".getBytes();
try {
 sockOut.write(buffer);
// write(buffer) writes all the bytes of the buffer.
sockOut.flush();
 // flush() should force the writing of the buffer content onto the float.
// Does not wait for the buffer to fill up.
 sockOut.write(buffer, 0, 2);
// write(buffer, pos, nbre) writes number of bytes (nbre) from the
indicated position (pos) .
} catch (IOException e) {}
```

The write and flush can raise a particular IOException, an attempt to write on a closed float.

In the following segment, we will transfer various data by passing through a single chain of characters:

```
try {
  OutputStream sockOut = socket.getOutputStream();
  byte[ ] buffer = new byte[1024];
  String envoi = "chain String"+" "+(-1234)+" "+12.34+" "+true;
  buffer = envoi.getBytes();
  sockOut.write(buffer, 0, envoi.length());
  sockOut.flush();
} catch (IOException e) {}
```

4.2.1.5. *Direct read the stream of a socket*

The following code allows a direct read of the stream of a socket:

```
InputStream sockIn = socket.getInputStream();
// Obtain the read InputStream of the socket.
byte[ ] buffer = new byte[1024];
int read;
try {
 read = sockIn.read(buffer);
```

```
// read the stream and store it into the buffer. Returns the number of read bytes.
System.out.write(buffer, 0, lu);
// display the buffer on the standard output.
} catch (IOException e) {}
```

The end of float can be normal (closed writing) or accidental (disconnection of end of writing process).

The reading operations can raise an IOException.

4.2.1.6. *High-level reading and writing*

DataOutputStream makes it possible to write any type of Java primitive on all systems.

The following code writes data in a known format in a socket:

```
DataOutputStream sockDataOut = null;
try {
sockDataOut = new DataOutputStream(socket.getOutputStream());
sockDataOut.writeByte(6); //writes the first byte of the number.
sockDataOut.writeChar('c'); //writes the character that corresponds to the first 2 bytes.
  sockDataOut.writeBoolean(true); //writes the Boolean on a byte.
  sockDataOut.writeInt(-1234); // writes the number on 4 bytes.
  sockDataOut.writeDouble(12.34); // writes the double on 8 bytes.
  sockDataOut.flush(); // should force write the content of the buffer onto the float, if there is a buffer.
  sockDataOut.writeUTF("chaine String"); // writes the String by encoding it into UTF-8 modified.
} catch (IOException e) {
}
```

For the reading of Java data in a known format from a socket, we must use DataInputStream that allows us to read any type of Java primitive on all systems.

```
DataInputStream sockDataIn = null;
try {
  sockDataIn = new DataInputStream(socket.getInputStream());
  byte by = sockDataIn.readByte(); // returns the next byte.
  char c = sockDataIn.readChar(); // returns the next character.
  boolean bo = sockDataIn.readBoolean();
// reads a byte and returns false if the byte is == 0.
  int i = sockDataIn.readInt(); // reads 4 bytes and returns the corresponding number.
  double d = sockDataIn.readDouble(); // reads 8 bytes and returns the corresponding double.
  String s = sockDataIn.readUTF(); // decodes the bytes into characters and returns the subsequent String.
} catch (EOFException e) {
} catch (IOException e) {
}
```

Any of the above methods raise EOFException if the end of the float is reached.

To write the text in a socket:

```
PrintWriter sockWriter = new PrintWriter(socket.getOutputStream()));
sockWriter.print("chaine String");
sockWriter.print(1234);
sockWriter.print(12.34);
sockWriter.println(true);
```

– We create a PrintWriter attached to the OutputStream.

– We can then directly read any Java type with print or println.

– None of these methods generate Exceptions.

The following code allows a user to read a socket's text line by line:

```
try{
BufferedReader sockReader = new BufferedReader(new InputStreamReader
(socket.getInputStream()))
```

```
String line;
while ((line = sockReader.readLine()) != null)    System.out.println(line);
} catch (IOException e) {}
```

– We create a BufferedReader attached to the InputStream.

– We can then directly read the chain of characters with readLine().

– readLine() returns the read line without the end character(s) and null if it reaches the end of float.

4.2.1.7. *Transmitting objects through the sockets*

In the following segment, we will discuss transmitting objects through the sockets.

Example: a client connects to a server to find out a student's major and grade.

– A table of students is stored on the server side.

– A client connects to the server and wishes to obtain a student's info.

– The client must send the name of the student to the server.

– The server reads the name, confirms receipt, browses the table to find the student and finally saves the student object.

– This object is sent to the client using the sockets.

– The object is read by the client (restore).

– The client displays the characteristics of the object.

– The object transmitted via the network must be serializable.

```
import java.io.Serializable;
public class Student implements Serializable{
  String name;
  String major;
  int moy;
```

```
    Student (String name, String major, int moy) {
      this.name = name;
      this.major = major;
      this.moy = moy;
    }
      String getNom() {
      return nom;
    }
    public String toString() {
      return "Student: "+name+"   "+major+" : "+moy;
    }
  }
```

The Student class is shared between the client and the server[1].

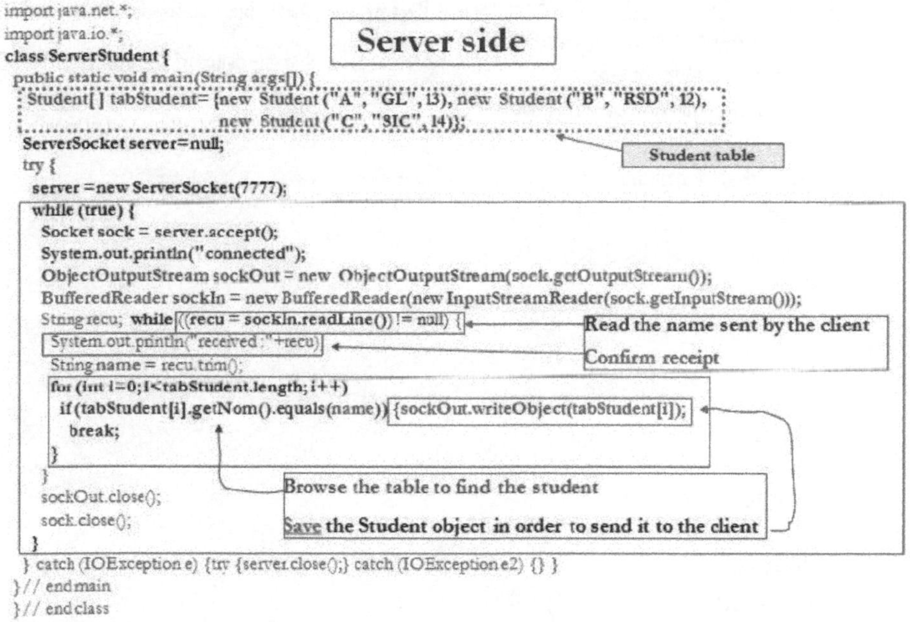

Server side

```
import java.net.*;
import java.io.*;
class ServerStudent {
 public static void main(String args[]) {
  Student[] tabStudent= {new Student ("A", "GL", 13), new Student ("B", "RSD", 12),
                         new Student ("C", "SIC", 14)};
  ServerSocket server=null;
  try {
   server =new ServerSocket(7777);
   while (true) {
    Socket sock = server.accept();
    System.out.println("connected");
    ObjectOutputStream sockOut = new ObjectOutputStream(sock.getOutputStream());
    BufferedReader sockIn = new BufferedReader(new InputStreamReader(sock.getInputStream()));
    String recu; while ((recu = sockIn.readLine()) != null) {
    System.out.println("received :"+recu);
     String name = recu.trim();
     for (int i=0;i<tabStudent.length;i++)
      if (tabStudent[i].getNom().equals(name)) {sockOut.writeObject(tabStudent[i]);
       break;
     }
    }
    sockOut.close();
    sock.close();
   }
  } catch (IOException e) {try {server.close();} catch (IOException e2) {} }
 }// endmain
}// endclass
```

Student table

Read the name sent by the client

Confirm receipt

Browse the table to find the student

Save the Student object in order to send it to the client

1 For a color version of the codes appearing in this chapter, see www.iste.co.uk/ benmammar/ java.zip

```
import java.io.*; import java.net.*;
public class ClientStudent {
 public static void main(String[] args) throws IOException {
 String hostName = "localhost";
  String NameStudent = "A";
  Socket sock = null;
  PrintWriter sockOut = null;
  ObjectInputStream sockIn = null;
  try {
   sock = new Socket(hostName, 7777);
   sockOut = new PrintWriter(sock.getOutputStream(), true);
   sockIn = new ObjectInputStream(sock.getInputStream());
  } catch (UnknownHostException e) {System.err.println("host cannot be reached : "+hostName); System.exit(1); }
   catch (IOException e) {System.err.println("cannot connect to: "+hostName); System.exit(1);}
  sockOut.println(NameStudent);
  try {
   Object recu = sockIn.readObject();
   if (recu == null) System.out.println("connection error");
   else { Student Student = (Student)recu;
    System.out.println("server -> client : " + Student);
   }
  } catch (ClassNotFoundException e) {System.err.println("Unknown class : "+hostName); System.exit(1);}
  sockOut.close();
  sockIn.close();
  sock.close();
 }
}
```

Client side

Send the name of the student to the server

Restore the student object received from the server

Display the characteristics of the student

Execution:

Server side:

connected
received: A

Client side:

server -> client: Student: A GL: 13

4.2.1.8. *Communications between a Java applet and a server using sockets*

The following execution shows a communication between an applet and a server using sockets:

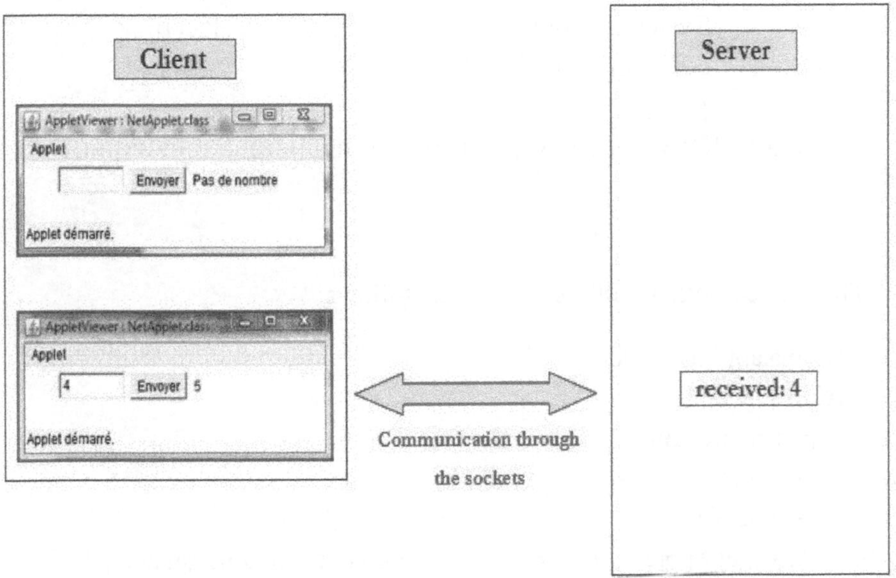

Figure 4.4. *Communication between an applet and a server with the Sockets. For a color version of the figure, see www.iste.co.uk/benmammar/java.zip*

The implementation of the server is as follows:

```
import java.io.*;
import java.net.*;
import java.util.*;
public class NetServer {
  public static void main(String[] args) {
        try{
              ServerSocket serverSocket = new ServerSocket(8765);
              Socket clientSocket = serverSocket.accept();
              BufferedReader in = new BufferedReader(new
```

```
                InputStreamReader(clientSocket.getInputStream()));
               PrintWriter out = new
                PrintWriter(clientSocket.getOutputStream(), true);
              while (true) {
              Integer numb =  new Integer(in.readLine());
              System.out.println("recu: " + numb.intValue());
              out.println(numb.intValue()+1);
              }
        }catch(IOException ex){System.err.println(ex);}
  }
}
```

The implementation of the client is as follows:

```
import java.applet.Applet;
import java.awt.*;
import java.awt.event.*;
import java.io.*;
import java.net.*;
public class NetApplet extends Applet implements ActionListener {
  TextField numbField;
  Label display;
  Socket socket;
  public void init() {
    try {
      socket = new Socket("localhost",8765);
    } catch (UnknownHostException e) {System.out.println("Unknown
host");}
      catch (IOException e) { System.out.println("IO Exception");}
    numbField = new TextField(6);
    add(numbField);
    Button button = new Button("Send");
    add(button);
      button.addActionListener(this);
      display = new Label("Pas de nombre");
```

```
        add(display);
    }
  public void actionPerformed(ActionEvent e)   {
     int numb = 0;
        String numbStr = null;
        BufferedReader in = null;
        PrintWriter out = null;
     String actionCommand = e.getActionCommand(); // know the source of
the event
     if (e.getSource() instanceof Button)
       if (actionCommand.equals("Send")){
                try {numb = Integer.parseInt(numbField.getText());}
                catch  (NumberFormatException  ex)  {System.out.println
("Number Format Exception");}
                try {
                in = new BufferedReader(new
                  InputStreamReader(socket.getInputStream()));
                out = new PrintWriter(socket.getOutputStream(), true);
                }
                catch     (IOException     ex)     {System.out.println("IO
Exception");}
                 out.println(numb);
                 try {numbStr = in.readLine();}
                catch (IOException ex) {System.out.println("Applet receive
                 failed:");}
                display.setText(numbStr);

       }
   }
}// end of class
```

4.2.2. *High-level communication: middleware*

These are layers offering more complex services. These layers are created using TCP/UDP layers.

Example: call from a method in a distant entity.

– The middleware is an intermediary layer (software layer) that fits into the communication infrastructure of a network and the elements of the distributed application.

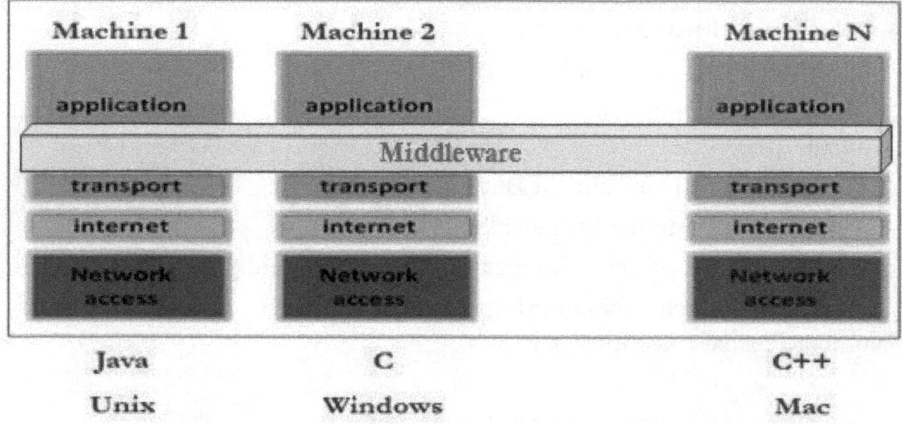

Figure 4.5. *Position of Middleware in a network. For a color version of the figure, see www.iste.co.uk/benmammar/java.zip*

– The distributed environments are based (for the most-part) on an RPC mechanism (remote procedure call).

– This mechanism functions with a request/response mode.

– The client makes a request (asks for a service).

– The server then processes the request and, finally, returns a response to the client.

The RPC possesses the following characteristics:

– Procedural programming, so not object-oriented.

– Parameters and return values are primitive type.

– No "distant reference".

Subsequently, middleware evolved in the following ways:

– JAVA RMI (Remote Method Invocation).

- Mono-language; Java, multiplatform: from JVM to JVM.

- CORBA (Common Object Request Broker Architecture).

- Multi-language, multiplatform.

- DCOM (Distributed Component Object Model) de Microsoft.

- Multi-language, communication between distributed software components.

In the following section, we will focus on Java RMI.

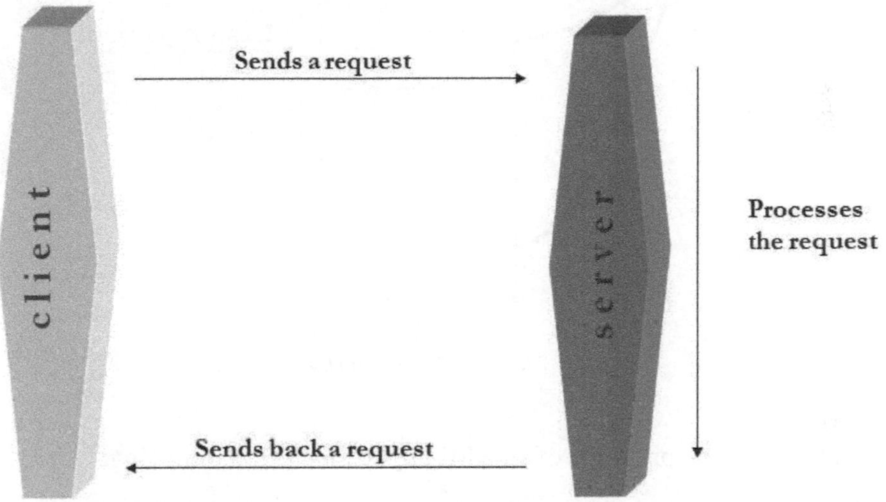

Figure 4.6. *RPC operation. For a color version of the figure, see www.iste.co.uk/benmammar/java.zip*

4.2.2.1. *Introduction to RMI*

RMI allows virtual Java machines to communicate whether they are on the same machine or on two distinct machines.

java.rmi: API integrated into the JDK 1.1 and more (since 1997).

In order for the clients to access distant services, they must be saved in a registry.

The RMI registry is called rmiregistry and it possesses a hashing table where the keys are names and the values are distant objects.

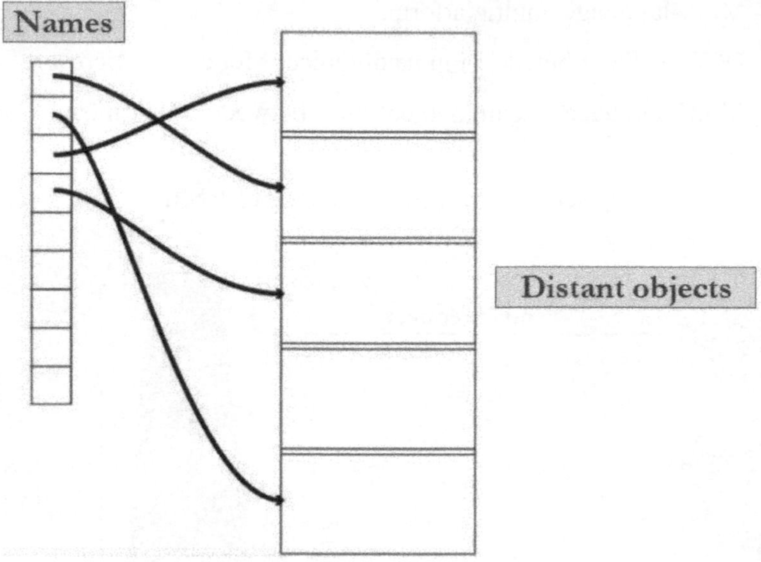

Figure 4.7. *rmiregistry*

The operating principle of an RMI application is the following:

– The server creates the objects and saves them in the rmiregistry.

– This allows the clients to locate the objects and get references towards these objects.

– When a client wishes to summon an object remotely, it checks the rmiregistry to locate the object: it supplies the name of the object and receives a reference towards this distant object (a stub).

– With the newly obtained reference, the client will be able to summon the methods of this object.

The methods of the proxy B summon the real methods on the distant object B by traveling over the network.

– When a client obtains a reference to a distributed object, it obtains in fact a reference to a stub.

– A stub is a proxy (local representative of a distant object) that is loaded into the client upon obtaining the reference.

– The client therefore summons, via its reference, the methods that reside in the stub that summons the real methods on the distant object by travelling over a network.

– This is the mechanism that ensures the transparency of calls.

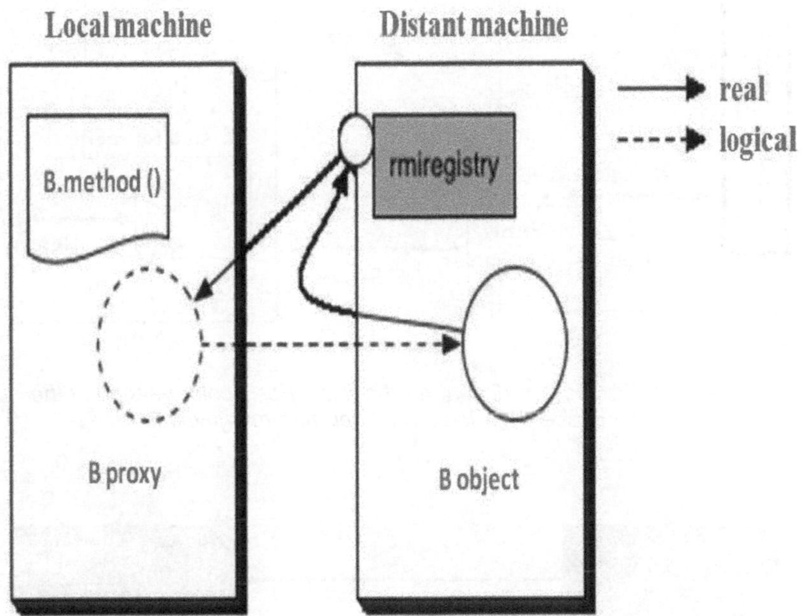

Figure 4.8. *Operation of an RMI application. For a color version of the figure, see www.iste.co.uk/benmammar/java.zip*

Figure 4.9 represents the stages of a call for a distant method.

4.2.2.2. *RMI architecture*

Figure 4.10 represents the RMI architecture.

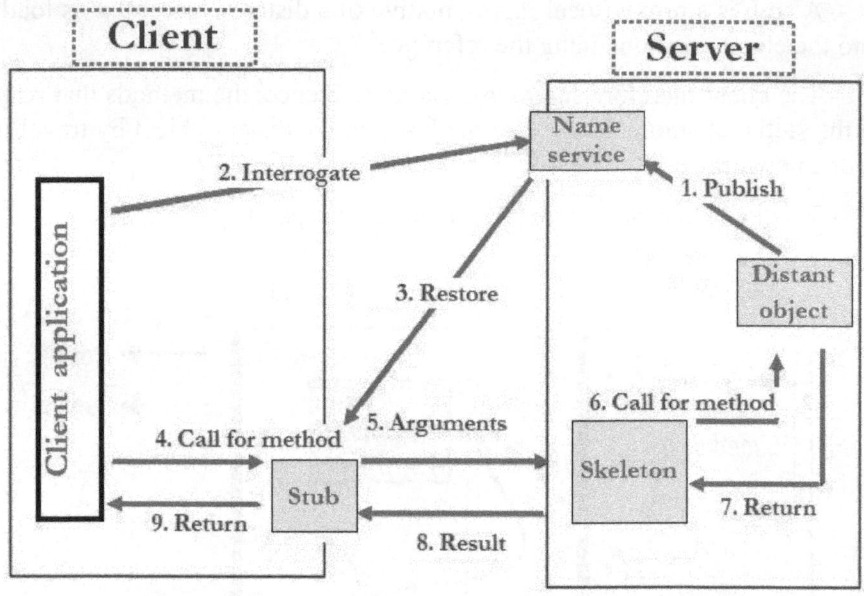

Figure 4.9. *Stages of a distant method call. For a color version of the figure, see www.iste.co.uk/benmammar/java.zip*

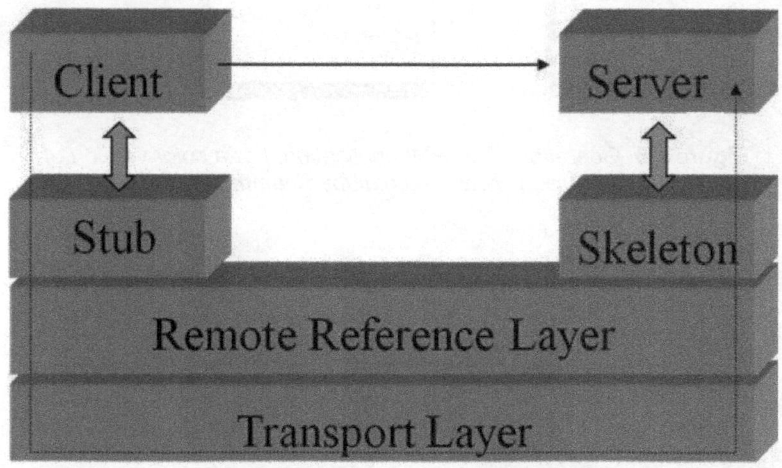

Figure 4.10. *RMI architecture. For a color version of the figure, see www.iste.co.uk/benmammar/java.zip*

– First layer: stub/skeleton.

- Stub: local representative of the distributed object.

- Initiates a connection with the distant JVM by transmitting the distant summon to the layer of reference objects (RRL).

- Assembles the parameters in preparation for their transfer to the distant JVM.

- Waits for the results of the remote invocation, disassembles the value or the exception returned and returns the value by calling it.

- Skeleton: used to locate the distributed object.

- Disassembles the parameters for the distant method.

- Calls on the requested method.

- Assembly of the result (returned value or exception) destined to the caller.

- Remarks: The skeleton is no longer necessary since Java 2 (1998).

- A similar class of generic skeleton is shared between all distant objects.

- Furthermore, up until version 5.0 of J2SE (2004), a stub compiler called RMIC (Java RMI Compiler) was required to generate the stub/ skeleton before saving on the RMI registry.

- Now, it is possible to generate them dynamically (no need to use the RMIC).

– Second layer: RRL (object reference layer).

- Helps obtain the reference of the distant object by consulting the rmiregistry.

- rmiregistry executes on each machine hosting distant objects.

- Only one rmiregistry per JVM.

- rmiregistry accepts service requests on port 1099 (by default).

– Third layer: transport.

- Uses a communication protocol above TCP/IP.

- During a method call, the stub transmits the call to the RRL layer, the latter transmits the request to the transport layer of the RMI that is above the TCP/IP and transfers the request by climbing up to the skeleton that calls upon the distant object.

- By default, RMI uses the protocol JRMP (Java Remote Method Protocol) on port 1099. This is a protocol that is used to call distant methods.

- JRMP is the communication protocol of RMI, used only between applications written in Java

- Original version.

- Integrated in the language.

- Simple to use.

- Starting from Java 2, and for compatibility with CORBA, communications between the client and the server can be performed using the protocol IIOP (Internet Inter-ORB Protocol).

- Recent version.

- Compatible with CORBA.

- More difficult to implement.

In this case, the package javax.rmi is required

4.2.2.3. *Deploying the RMI*

A number of packages are used to deploy RMI:

– java.rmi.Naming

– java.rmi.Remote

– java.rmi.RemoteException

– java.rmi.server.UnicastRemoteObject

– java.rmi.registry.LocateRegistry

– java.rmi.NotBoundException

java.rmi.Naming: is a final class: public final class Naming extends Object.

– The server can record a distant object using the bind() (or rebind()) method.

– static void bind (String name, Remote obj) throws AlreadyBoundException, MalformedURLException, RemoteException.

– static void rebind (String name, Remote obj) throws RemoteException, MalformedURLException.

– Note: bind() throws an exception if an object is already recorded under the same name in the registry (same name for two different objects).

Remote is an interface for designing distant objects.

– The client will find the object thanks to the lookup() method.

– static Remote lookup (String name) throws NotBoundException, MalformedURLException, RemoteException

The following will deploy RMI:

– Server side:

- The definition of an interface containing the methods that can be called remotely (the interface is shared with the client).

- Writing a class that implements this interface.

- Writing a class (server) that will instance the object and record it while giving it a name in the RMI registry.

– Client side:

- Obtaining a reference on the distant object from its name.

- Calling method from that reference.

To deploy RMI, follow the steps given below:

Shared interface between the client and the server:

The interface must extend java.rmi.Remote.

```
import java.rmi.Remote;
import java.rmi.RemoteException;
    public interface Hello extends Remote {
     public String Bonjour() throws RemoteException;
    }
```

– Remote is a methodless interface.

– An object that implements the Hello interface is an object that supports distant access to its methods.

– All methods must launch a RemoteException.

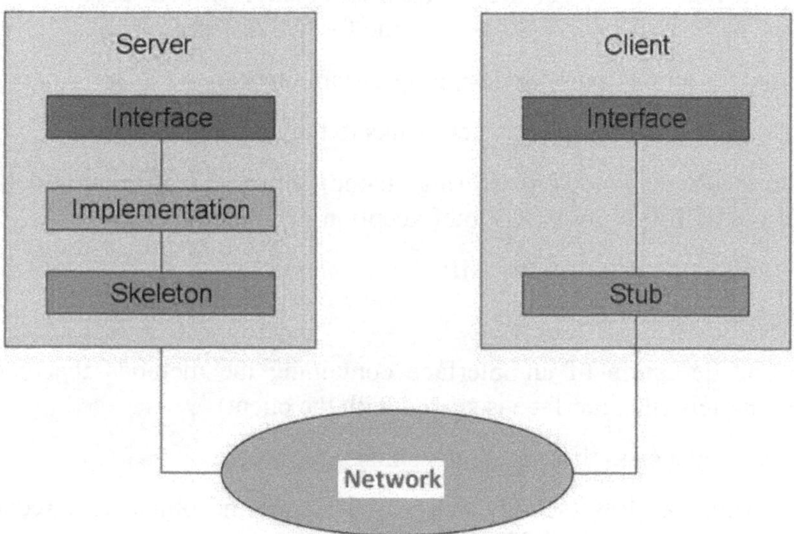

Figure 4.11. *Deploying RMI. For a color version of the figure, see www.iste.co.uk/benmammar/java.zip*

Implementing the class that implements the interface on the server side:

```
import java.rmi.RemoteException;
import java.rmi.server.UnicastRemoteObject;
public class HelloImpl extends UnicastRemoteObject implements Hello
{
    public HelloImpl() throws RemoteException {
    }
public String Bonjour() throws RemoteException {
      return "Bonjour tous le monde !";
    }
}
```

– It must implement the Hello interface.

– It must extend the UnicastRemoteObject.

– Unicast: the distant object exists in one unique copy on one single machine.

– It can implement methods other than the one in the interface, but these will not be remotely accessible.

– The builders launch a RemoteException.

– Therefore, the user must always write one.

Implementing the server:

```
import java.net.MalformedURLException;
import java.rmi.Naming;
import java.rmi.RemoteException;
import java.rmi.registry.LocateRegistry;
public class HelloServer {
  public static void main(String[] args) {
  try {
LocateRegistry.createRegistry(1099);
  } catch (RemoteException e1) {
     System.err.println("rmiregistry is already launched on this port");
     System.exit(1);
  }
      Hello hello;
      try {
         hello = new HelloImpl();
         Naming.rebind("rmi://localhost:1099/Hello",hello);
      } catch (RemoteException e) {
         System.err.println("have you launched rmiregistry?");
      System.exit(1);
      } catch (MalformedURLException e) {
```

```
            throw new InternalError("the URL is incorrect");
        }
      }
    }
```

The general format of an RMI URL is rmi://host:port/Nom.

Example: Naming.rebind("rmi://localhost:1099/Hello",hello).

– Only the Name is mandatory.

– The protocol by default is rmi.

– The default port is 1099.

– The default host is localhost.

Examples of valid URLs:

– Name (port 1099 on localhost).

– //172.16.2.125/Name (port = 1099).

– //172.16.2.125:2000/Name.

Implementing the client:

```
import java.net.MalformedURLException;
import java.rmi.Naming;
import java.rmi.NotBoundException;
import java.rmi.RemoteException;
public class HelloClient {
  public static void main(String[] args) {
    String url = null;
    Hello hello = null;
    try {
      url = "rmi://localhost:1099/Hello";
      hello = (Hello) Naming.lookup(url); // hello is the Stub
} catch (MalformedURLException e) {
      System.err.println("The URL " + url + "is incorrect");
System.exit(1);
    } catch (RemoteException e) {
```

```
            System.err.println("Have you launched the rmiregistry ?");
            System.exit(2);
        } catch (NotBoundException e) {
            System.err.println("Have you launched the server?");
            System.exit(2);
        }
    try {
            System.out.println(hello.Hello()); // call remote method
        } catch (RemoteException e) {
            System.err.println("The server appears to be down");
            System.exit(4);
        }
    }
}
```

– Launch server.

– Launch client.

– Execution on client side:

Bonjour tout le monde !

To implement an RMI application, you must first:

– Write the Remote interface(s).

- Hello.java.

– Write its (their) implementation(s).

- HelloImpl.java.

– Write the server.

- HelloServer.java.

– Write the client.

- HelloClient.java.

Note: it is possible to regroup both classes (server and interface implementation) in the same class.

The following example discusses this type of case. It is a remote multiplication.

The interface:

```
import java.rmi.Remote;
import java.rmi.RemoteException;
public interface Hello extends Remote {
public int multi (int a, int b) throws RemoteException;
}
```

Implementing the server:

```
import java.rmi.*;
import java.rmi.server.*;
import java.rmi.registry.*;
public class HelloServer extends UnicastRemoteObject implements
Hello {
public HelloServer() throws RemoteException {}
public int multi(int a, int b) throws RemoteException {
return a * b; }
public static void main(String[] args) {
    try {
    LocateRegistry.createRegistry(1099);
  } catch (RemoteException e1) {
     System.err.println("rmiregistry is already launched on this port");
     System.exit(1);
  }
   try {
HelloServer objet = new HelloServer();
Naming.rebind("badr",object);
System.out.println("Server ready");
}
```

```
catch(Exception e) {
System.err.println("Error: " + e.getMessage());
}
}
}
```

A few notes surrounding bind and rebind:

The following code is correct:

```
HelloServer object = new HelloServer();
Naming.rebind("badr",object);
Naming.rebind("badr1",object);
```

There is the possibility to attribute more than one name to the same object: bind or rebind regardless.

The following code generates an exception:

```
HelloServer object = new HelloServer();
HelloServer object1 = new HelloServer();
Naming.bind("badr",object);
Naming.bind("badr",object1);
```

The following code is correct:

```
HelloServer object = new HelloServer();
HelloServer object1 = new HelloServer();
Naming.rebind("badr",object);
Naming.rebind("badr",object1);
```

It works with a rebind because it is a resave; badr only refers to object1.

Implementing the client:

```
import java.rmi.*;
public class HelloClient {
public static void main(String[] args) {
try {
```

```
      Hello reference = (Hello)Naming.lookup("badr");
      int resultat = reference.multi(5,12);
     System.out.println("The multiplication is: " + result); }
   catch(Exception e) { System.err.println("Error: " + e.getMessage()); }
   }
   }
```

Execution:

– Server side: Server ready.

– Client side: The multiplication is 60.

The following class is useful for generating the registry:

– public final class LocateRegistry extends Object.

– Class used to generate the rmiregistry in the package java.rmi.registry.

– createRegistry method:

- static Registry createRegistry (int port): create registry.

- LocateRegistry.createRegistry(1099): create registry on port 1099.

- createRegistry is a static method that returns a Registry.

- public interface Registry extends Remote.

- In the package java.rmi.registry.

- LocateRegistry.createRegistry(1099): create a distant registry (rmiregistry).

– getRegistry method:

- Returns a reference towards the distant registry.

- Various signatures:

- static Registry getRegistry().

- static Registry getRegistry(int port).

- static Registry getRegistry(String host).

- static Registry getRegistry(String host, int port).

- static Registry getRegistry(String host, int port, RMIClientSocketFactory csf)

Example of application:

String [ ] NamesSaved = LocateRegistry.getRegistry("localhost", 1099).list();
liste (): method of the Registry interface which returns the list of names recorded in the registry.

4.2.2.4. *Parameter exchanges in RMI*

The parameters exchanged through the Java RMI must be:

– *Primitive types:* int, short, double, boolean …, also String.

– *Serializable objects.*

– *Remote objects.*

The primitive types are transmitted by value (copy).

The Serializable objects are serialized, transmitted, then deserialized (transmitted by value).

The Remote objects are transmitted under the form of distant references.

– *Primitive types:*

The following code represents the implementation of the method “multi” on the server side:

```
public int multi (int a, int b) throws RemoteException {
        return a * b;
}
```

The method call on the client side is as follows:

```
try {
   Hello reference = (Hello)Naming.lookup("badr");
   int result = reference.multi(5,12);
   System.out.println("The multiplication is: " + result);
}catch(Exception e) { System.err.println("Error: " + e.getMessage()); }
```

In the previous example, the call is performed by value.

– *Transmitting a Serializable object:*

Example: we wish to use a data server to store a set of 2D coordinates describing the positions of a certain number of vehicles on a plane.

This server will have to include the following functionalities:

– Creating a new position and attributing it a name.

– Read-access to the positions.

– Access to the number of positions.

– The server must implement a hashing-Table.

– In java, the Hashtable class is the one found in the package java.util.

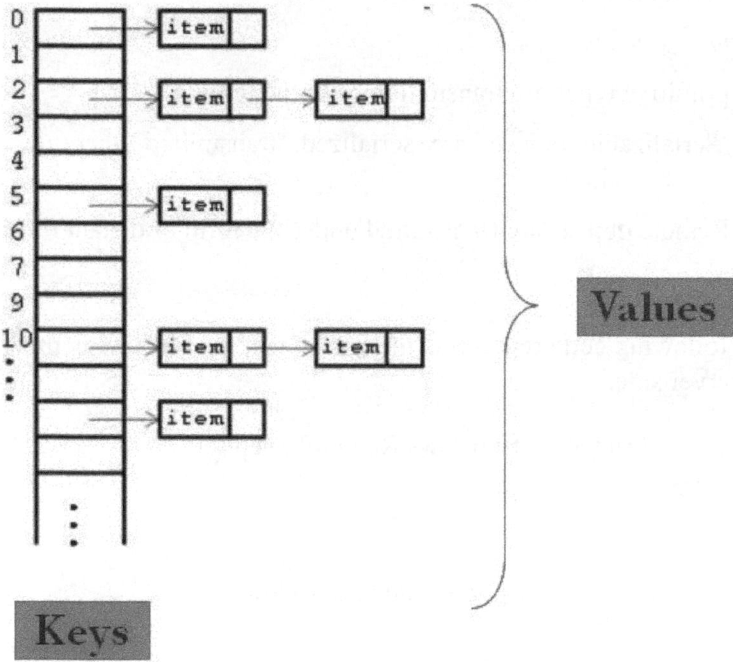

Figure 4.12. *rmiregistry. For a color version of the figure, see www.iste.co.uk/benmammar/java.zip*

In our case:

– The keys are the names given to the positions.

– The values are the 2D coordinates of the vehicles.

– The shared interface is as follows:

```
import java.rmi.*;
 public interface Position extends Remote {
  public void insererTable (Point p, String nom) throws RemoteException;
  public Point position (String nom) throws RemoteException ;
  public int nombreCles() throws RemoteException ;
}
```

The previous interface implements the following:

– Creating a new position and attributing a name.

– Read-access to the positions.

– Access to the number of positions.

The Point class must implement Serializable.

```
import java.io.Serializable ;
public class Point implements Serializable {
  public float x;
  public float y;
  public Point(float xx,float yy) {
    x = xx;
    y = yy;
  }
public String toString() {
    return("("+x+", "+y+")") ;
  }
}
```

The implementation of the server:

```
import java.rmi.*;
import java.rmi.server.*;
import java.net.*;
import java.util.Hashtable;
import java.rmi.registry.*;
public class Serveur extends UnicastRemoteObject implements Position
{
 private Hashtable h;
public Serveur() throws RemoteException {
   h = new Hashtable() ;
  }
 public void insererTable(Point p,String nom) throws RemoteException
{
       h.put(nom,p);
  }
public Point position(String nom) throws RemoteException {
   return((Point) h.get(nom));
  }
 public int nombreCles() throws RemoteException {
   return(h.size());
  }
public static void main(String [] args) {
   try {
     Serveur ib = new Serveur();
             try {
LocateRegistry.createRegistry(1099);
  } catch (RemoteException e1) {
     System.err.println("rmiregistry is already launched on this port");
     System.exit(1);
  }
    Naming.rebind("rmi://localhost:1099/Data",ib);
    System.out.println("Ready"); }
   catch (RemoteException re) {
```

```
    System.out.println(re) ; }
   catch(MalformedURLException e) {
    System.out.println(e) ; }
  }
}
```

The implementation of the client:

```
import java.rmi.* ;
 public class Client {
  public static void main(String [] args) {
   try {
    Position b =(Position) Naming.lookup("Data");
    System.out.println(b.nombreCles()) ;
    b.insererTable(new Point(11,5),"P0") ;
    b.insererTable(new Point(14,9),"P1");
    System.out.println(b.nombreCles());
    System.out.println(b.position("P0")) ;
    System.out.println(b.position("P1")) ;
   }
   catch (Exception e) {
    System.out.println(e) ; }
  }
 }
```

Execution:

– Server side:

Ready

– Client side:

0
2
(11.0, 5.0)
(14.0, 9.0)

Ignoring Serializable in the Point definition as follows:

```
public class Point {
  public float x ;
  public float y ;
  public Point(float xx,float yy) {
    x = xx;
    y = yy;
  }
public String toString() {
    return("("+x+", "+y+")") ;
  }
}
```

will give us the following execution:

– Server side:

Ready // The transmission has not yet occurred.

– Client side:

0 // primitive type int does not pose a problem.

java.rmi.MarshalException: error marshalling arguments; nested exception is:

java.io.NotSerializableException: Position

The problem occurs for the Point type object transmission which must be Serializable.

Transmitting Remote objects: RMI multi-thread servers (chatrooms):

– Each client is a thread and has three possible actions: join, talk or leave.

– The server must now maintain a list of distributed objects (Remote).

– Use synchronized to guarantee coherence across the data.

– The client's actions must be displayed to other clients.

– Thread implemented using Jframe (Swing)

First client:

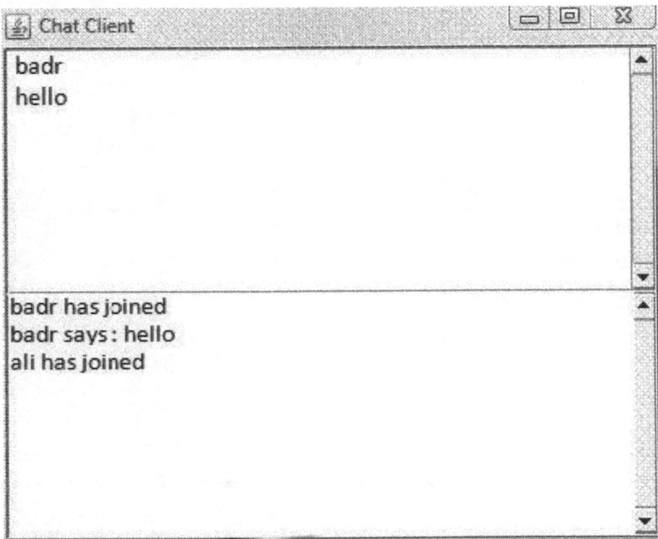

Second client:

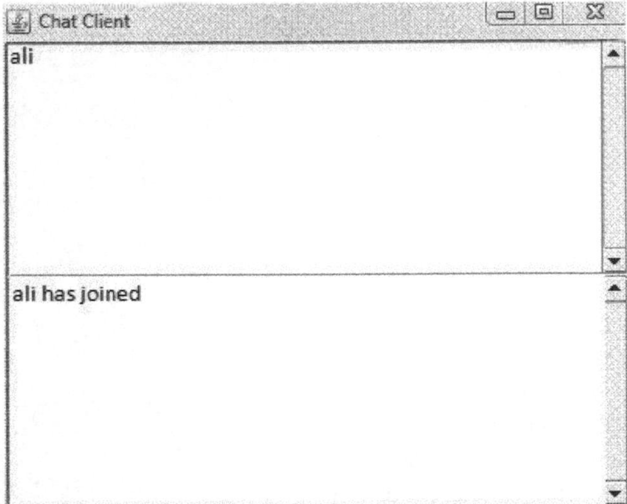

Third client:

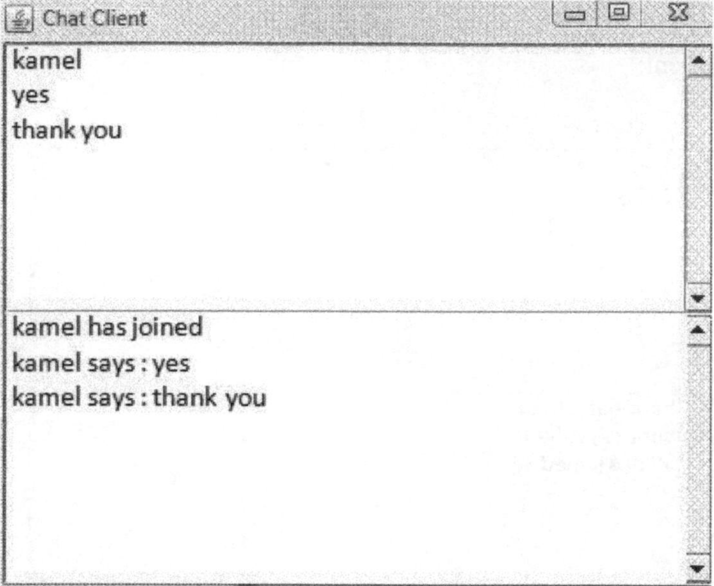

When the third client disconnects, the first client should see this:

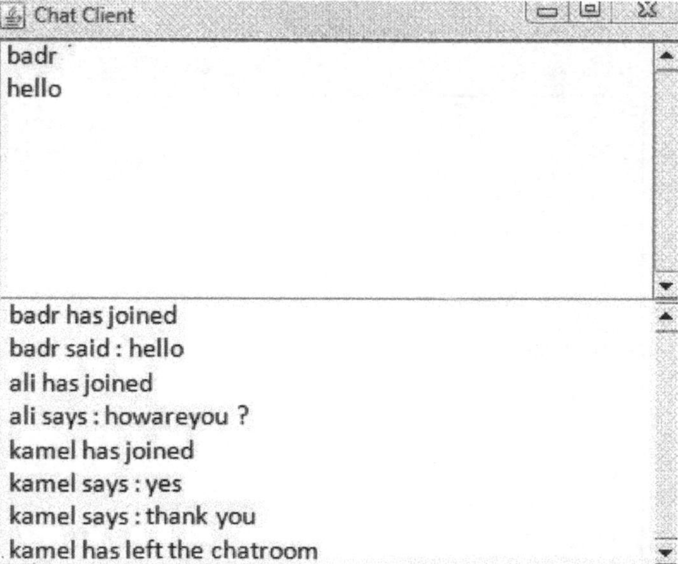

The second client will be as follows:

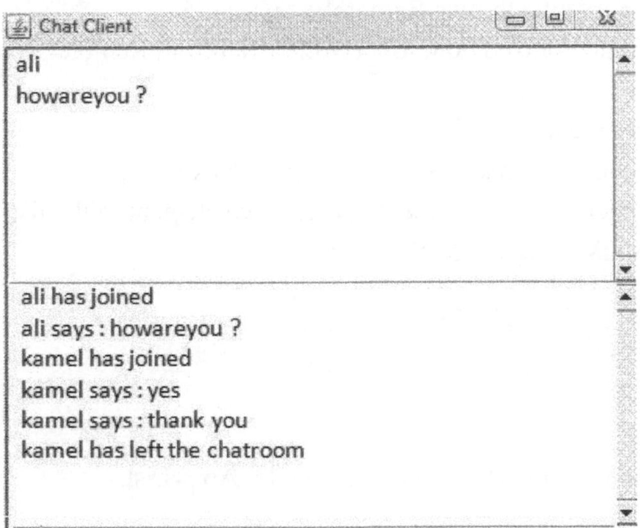


```
import java.rmi.*;
public interface ChatInterface extends Remote {
   public void rejoindre (Notify n) throws RemoteException;
   public void parler (Notify n, String s) throws RemoteException;
   public void laisser (Notify n) throws RemoteException;
}
import java.rmi.*;
public interface Notify extends Remote { // Notify refers to a client
   public String getName() throws RemoteException;
   public void setName(String s) throws RemoteException;
   public void joinMessage (String name) throws RemoteException;
   public void sendMessage (String name, String message) throws
RemoteException;
   public void exitMessage (String name) throws RemoteException;
} // name is the name of the client.
```

On the server side:

```
public class Serveur extends UnicastRemoteObject implements
ChatInterface {
```

```
private Collection<Notify> threadList = new ArrayList<Notify>();
 public Serveur() throws RemoteException {}
public synchronized void join (Notify n) throws RemoteException {
threadList.add(n);
// browse the list
for (Iterator i = threadList.iterator();i.hasNext(); ) {
Notify client = (Notify)i.next(); // retrieve element in the list
client.joinMessage(n.getName());
            }
   }
...
...
```

Collection is an interface implemented by ArrayList.

iterator() is a Collection method that returns an Iterator on the table (Iterator is an interface to designate an iterator on the table).
hasNext() and next() are methods of the Iterator.

Part of the class that implements Notify:

```
import java.rmi.*;
import java.rmi.server.*;
import javax.swing.JTextArea;

public class Message extends UnicastRemoteObject implements Notify {

    private javax.swing.JTextArea textArea;
    private String name;

    public Message(JTextArea ta) throws RemoteException {
            textArea = ta;
    }

    public void joinMessage(String name)throws RemoteException
    {
        try {textArea.append(name + " has joined\n");}
        catch(Exception e){System.out.println("error");}
    }
```

4.2.2.5. *Security management in RMI*

Security is important when code is downloaded (it can be risky to execute code from a remote server). Being able to transmit executable code remotely is, in theory, a security flaw. When transmitting code locally, there is no security issue.

– *Solution:*

- Implement a “security manager”.

– *General solution in Java:*

- Use class java.lang.SecurityManager (extends Object).

- This allows the specification of permissions to access files, networks, etc.

– *Specific solution for RMI:*

- Use class java.rmi.RMISecurityManager.

- public class RMISecurityManager extends SecurityManager.

With RMI, there are two ways to manage security:

– Use a sub-class of SecurityManager instead of RMISecurityManager.

```
public class SecurityManagerOuvert extends SecurityManager{
public void checkPermission(Permission perm) { }
}
```

– Use RMISecurityManager in conjunction with (from Java 2) a file describing permissions policy: file “java.policy”.

The file java.policy defines the security policy in order to specify authorized actions.

In: C:\Program Files (x86)\Java\jdk1.8.0_25\jre\lib\security.

Example of content in the file java.policy:

```
grant {
 permission java.security.AllPermission;
};
```

It allows all method calls (no security policy).

```
grant {
permission java.net.SocketPermission "*:1024-65535", "connect, accept";
permission java.net.SocketPermission "*:80", "connect";
permission java.io.FilePermission "C:\\temp\\m2rsd.txt", "read";
permission java.io.FilePermission "C:\\temp\\test.exe ", "read, write, delete, execute";
};
```

It allows socket connections on ports 1024 to 65535 for all RMI clients and connections to the default Webserver (port 80) on all machines. It also defines access rights in relation to cited files.

To install a security manager, execute the following code: System.setSecurityManager(new SecurityManager()));

Example:

```
public static void main (String args[]) { // server
System.setSecurityManager (new SecurityManager ()) ;
try {
LocateRegistry.createRegistry(1099);
  } catch (RemoteException e1) {
    System.err.println("rmiregistry is already launched on this port");
    System.exit(1);
  }
```

To use java.policy:

```
$ javac Server.java
$ java -Djava.security.policy=java.policy Server
```

We can also use RMI with TLS:

– Transport Layer Security (TLS), previously known as Secure Sockets Layer (SSL), is a security protocol for exchanges over the Internet.

– Since J2SE 5.0 (2004), it is possible to use TLS with RMI.

– TLS acts as an additional layer that ensures data-security, located between the application layer and the transport layer.

Objective:

– Server authentication.

– Optionally, client authentication.

– Data confidentiality (or encrypted session).

– Integrity of exchanged data.

– The JSSE API (Java Secure Socket Extension) makes it possible to manipulate secure sockets in Java responding to SSL specifications.

– The JSSE classes and interfaces are grouped into packages javax.net and javax.net.ssl.

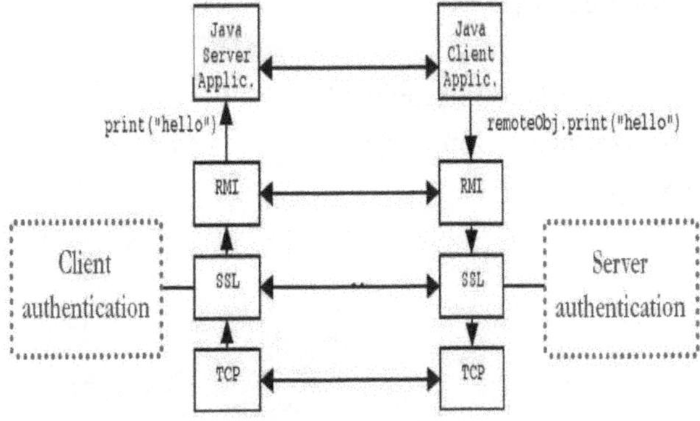

Figure 4.13. *RMI with TLS. For a color version of the figure, see www.iste.co.uk/benmammar/java.zip*

4.2.2.6. *Dynamic class loading*

– Java classes are hosted on a Web server.

– This avoids holding all class definitions locally.

– The same class files are shared by all clients.

– Only classes that are needed are loaded.

– In this case, we can turn towards dynamic loading:

- Place the java class (stub, for example) in a Web server that is accessible by the client. For example: http://monserveur.fr/test.

- Implement a SecurityManager:

- Add the following line in the client and the server: System.setSecurityManager(new SecurityManager()));

- Execute the following on the server: java -Djava.security.policy=java.policy Server

- Execute the client by supplying the dynamic class loading URL:

- java -Djava.rmi.server.codebase=http://myserver.fr/test/

- Djava.security.policy=java.policy Client

The stub on the server side is as follows:

```
import java.rmi.Naming;
public class HelloClient {
public HelloClient() {
try {
Hello obj = (Hello)Naming.lookup("Hello");
System.out.println(obj.Bonjour());
} catch (Exception e) {
```

```
System.out.println("HelloClient exception: " + e);
}
}
}
```

HelloClient.java is a class shared between various RMI clients.

The following code represents an RMI client using dynamic class loading:

```
import java.rmi.server.RMIClassLoader;
import java.util.Properties;
public class DynamicClient {
public DynamicClient() throws Exception {
// Install a security manager (without this manager, loading is unauthorized)
System.setSecurityManager(new SecurityManager());
Properties p = System.getProperties();
/Indicate the download path
String url = p.getProperty("java.rmi.server.codebase");
// Download desired class
Class clientClass = RMIClassLoader.loadClass(url, "HelloClient");
// Create an instance of class
clientClass.newInstance();
}
public static void main (String args[]) {
try {DynamicClient dc = new DynamicClient();
} catch (Exception e) {System.out.println(e);}
}
}
```

4.2.2.7. *Asynchronicity in RMI: callback methods*

In RMI, the client calls a method located on the server side.

Requirement: during execution, the server can launch processes on the client side.

Perform a call from the server towards the clients.

Objective: increase dynamism.

In this case, each element (client or server) can play both roles indifferently (client and server simultaneously).

Server calls towards the client are called callbacks.

– Since the server does not know the way this type of method is implemented and that its execution time can be long, the callbacks will generally be implemented as asynchronous operations.

– The server avoids penalizing the other clients with a synchronous call.

– Synchronous call → Blocked execution awaiting result.

– The callback is a mechanism that allows the introduction of asynchronicity in RMI, whose invocations are naturally synchronous and blocking.

– An asynchronous method is always void (returns no result).

– The program making the call does not need an immediate result; if not, it will be blocked.

– In Java methods are synchronous except for the start() method of a thread.

– start() does not block the calling thread.

– The client passes the object to callback (Remote object) as a parameter to the server.

– The client leaves its coordinates to be called back subsequently.

– First interface: ServerInterface (server side implementation).

– The server executes an asynchronous call on the object.

– A thread must perform the callback.

– Second interface: InterfaceCallback (client side implementation).

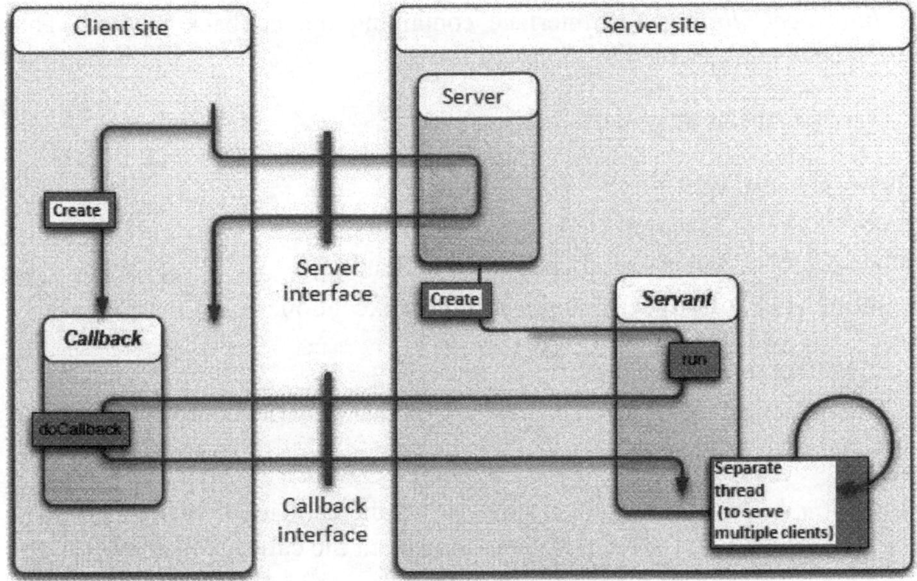

Figure 4.14. *Callback in RMI. For a color version of the figure, see www.iste.co.uk/benmammar/java.zip*

To perform the callback, we need six classes as follows:

Client.java	Server.java
InterfaceServer.java	**InterfaceServer.java**
Callback.java	Servant.java
InterfaceCallback.java	**InterfaceCallback.java**

Figure 4.15. *Necessary classes for a callback. For a color version of the figure, see www.iste.co.uk/benmammar/java.zip*

InterfaceCalback.java: interface containing the callback method. This interface is implemented by *Callback.java.*

An example of this interface is as follows:

```
import java.rmi.Remote ;
import java.rmi.RemoteException ;
public interface InterfaceCallback extends Remote {
   public void doCallback () throws RemoteException ;
}
```

It is the interface of the callback method that is implemented on the client side.

Callback.java: the class that implements the callback method. This class is available only on the client side to implement the callback method.

```
import java.rmi.RemoteException ;
import java.rmi.server.UnicastRemoteObject ;
public class Callback extends UnicastRemoteObject implements
InterfaceCallback {
public Callback ( ) throws RemoteException {}
public void doCallback () throws RemoteException {
   System.out.println ("Bonjour tous le monde") ;
}
}
```

Servant.java: the thread which launches the callback method.

```
import java.rmi.*;
public class Servant extends Thread {
private InterfaceCallback obj ;
public Servant (InterfaceCallback obj) {
this.obj = obj ;
}
public void run ( ) { // execution as a separate thread
try {Thread.sleep (3000) ; } catch ( InterruptedException e ) { }
```

```
try {obj.doCallback () ; // executes the callback, calls the method on the client side
}
catch (RemoteException e ) {
   System.err.println ("Return call failed: " + e ) ;
}
}
}
```

InterfaceServer.java: interface containing the method used by the server in order to call back the client, the parameter of this method is the object to call back. This interface is implemented by *Server.java.*

```
import java.rmi.Remote;
import java.rmi.RemoteException;
public interface InterfaceServeur extends Remote {
  public void callMeBack (InterfaceCallback  obj) throws RemoteException
;
}
```

The callMeBack method is used by the client.

Client.java: creates the object and passes it to the server (call the method of the InterfaceServer that is implemented on the server side).

Make a classic RMI to be called back:

```
import java.rmi.Naming ;
public class Client {
public static void main( String [ ] args ) throws Exception {
Callback  obj = new Callback ( ) ; // creation of the callback object
InterfaceServeur serv= (InterfaceServeur) Naming.lookup ("Server");
System.out.println ("Starting call");
serv.callMeBack (obj) ; // call request
}
}
```

Server.java: implements the method that calls back the client passing the received object of this last thread.

```
import java.rmi.Naming;
import java.rmi.RemoteException;
import java.rmi.registry.LocateRegistry;
import java.rmi.server.UnicastRemoteObject;
public class Server extends UnicastRemoteObject implements
InterfaceServer {
public Server ( ) throws RemoteException { }
public void callMeBack (InterfaceCallback obj) throws RemoteException {
Servant servant = new Servant (obj) ; // Creation of the thread
servant.start ( ) ; // Initialization of the thread
}
public static void main( String [ ] args ) throws Exception {
try {LocateRegistry.createRegistry(1099);} catch (RemoteException e1) {
    System.err.println("rmiregistry is already launched on this
port");System.exit(1); }
Server serv = new Server ( ) ;
Naming.rebind ("Server" , serv) ;
System.out.println ("Server ready" ) ;
}
}
```

Execution:

Server side: server ready.

Client side: starting call.

Hello everyone.

4.2.2.8. *Distributed garbage collector in RMI*

– Difficulty: distributed environment so remote references.

– Goal: prevent referencing message losses.

A distant object is made available for the DGC (distributed garbage collector), if there are no more stubs present.

– With RMI: double mechanism managed by:

- *Reference counting:* number of clients counting the object.

  - Each reference transmission +1.

  - Each end of referencing –1.

- *Lease:* Memory that is "let" to an object for a limited time.

  - By default 600000 milliseconds (10 min), changeable with the property java.rmi.dgc.leaseValue (starting in version 1.1 of the JDK).

  - To modify it, do it upon launching the program:

$ java -Djava.rmi.dgc.leaseValue=20000 Server.

If the counter falls below 0 or if the lease expires, the object becomes a candidate for the DGC.

Appendix

Exercise 1: lifecycle of a thread

Consider the following class:

```
class Parrot4 extends Thread{
 private String cri = null;
 private int fois = 0;
 public Parrot4 (String s, int i)  {
  cri = s;
  fois = i;}
 public void run() {
  System.out.println("Thread parrot:"
     + Thread.currentThread().getName());
  for (int n=0; n<fois; n++) {
   try {  Thread.sleep(1000); }
   catch(InterruptedException e) { }
   System.out.println(cri);
  }
 }
}

class ChatAndLaunchParrot4{
 public static void main(String args[]) {
  Parrot4 parrot = new Parrot4("coco",5);
```

```
    parrot.start();
    System.out.println("Thread chatty : "
        + Thread.currentThread().getName());
    for (int n=0; n<15; n++) {
      try { Thread.sleep(1000);}
      catch(InterruptedException e) { }
      System.out.print("Thread parrot isAlive: "+ parrot.isAlive()+"\t");
            blabla();
    }
  }
  private static void blabla() {
    System.out.println("blabla");
  }
}
```

Question: Launch the execution of the above program.

What is the name of the primary thread, what is the name given by default to the other thread? What is the point of the isAlive() method? *Hint*: the class method currentThread() returns a pointer on the object Thread, which calls this method.

Exercise 2: properties of different threads

Consider the following two classes:

```
class Parrot5 extends Thread {
  private String cri = null;
  private int fois = 0;
  public Parrot5(String s, int i)  {
    super("parrot");
    cri = s;
    fois = i;
}
public void run(){
    afficheThreads();
```

```
  for (int n=0; n<fois; n++) {
   try {  Thread.sleep(1000);  }
   catch(InterruptedException e) { }
   System.out.println(cri) }
  afficheThreads(); }
 private void afficheThreads() {
  Thread[] tabThread = new Thread[Thread.activeCount()];
  int nbrThread =  Thread.enumerate(tabThread);
  for (int i = 0; i < nbrThread ; i++)
    System.out.println(i + "-ieme Thread: " + tabThread[i].getName());
 }
}

class ChatAndLaunchParrot5 {
 public static void main(String args[]) {
  Thread.currentThread().setName("chatty");
  Parrot5 parrot = new Parrot5("coco",15);
  parrot.start();
  for (int n=0; n<5; n++) {
   try { Thread.sleep(1000); }
   catch(InterruptedException e) { }
   blabla();
            }
            }
 private static void blabla() {
  System.out.println("blabla");
 }
 }
```

Hint: The method setName (String name) makes it possible to name a thread. The Thread builder offers the possibility to name it as follows: Thread (String name).

The class method activeCount () gives the number of active threads in the calling thread's group.

The class method enumerates (Thread[] table) stores in the given table the references of the active threads in the calling thread's group and sub-groups. It returns the number of active threads obtained.

Question: launch the execution of the previous program.

The procedure displayThreads() is called before and after the loop for the method run().
The active threads before the loop were:
Number 0 Thread: chatty
1st Thread: parrot
After the loop for, they became:
Number 0 Thread: parrot
1st Thread: DestroyJavaVM

Explain this result, what is DestroyJavaVM?

Exercise 3: four counters in parallel

The objective for this exercise is to create four counters executing in parallel.

Each "counter" has a name (Toto for example) and it counts from 1 to 10. It pauses randomly between each number (0 to 5000 milliseconds for example). Each counter displays a number (for example, Toto will display, "Toto: 3"); n displays a message such as "Toto has finished counting to 10" when it has finished.

The counter class possesses one single attribute, which is the name of the String-type counter.

Write the counter class and test it by launching 4 that count up to 10. See which one finishes first (the four counters are named Tata, Titi, Toto, Tutu).

Make 2 versions: one where the threads are created with a Thread daughter-class, and one where they are created with an instance of a separate class that implements Runnable.

Exercise 4: resource in mutual exclusion

Consider the following three java classes:

```
public class Printer1 {
 private String text;
 public Printer1() {
   text="";
}
 public void print(String t) {
   text=t;
   for (int j=0;j<text.length()-1; j++) {
   System.out.print(text.charAt(j));
     try { Thread.sleep(100);}
    catch (InterruptedException e) {};
   } // end for
System.out.println(text.charAt(text.length()-1));
 }
}

public class Prog56 {
 public static void main (String argv[]) {
   Writer2 writerA, writerB;
   Printer1 print= new Printer1();
   writerA = new Writer2("ABC", print);
   writerB = new Writer2("XYZ", print);
   writerA.start();
   writerB.start();
 }
}

public class Writer2 extends Thread {
 private String text;
 private Printer1 print;
 public Writer2(String t, Printer1 i) {
   print=i;
```

```
    text=t;
  }

  public void run() {
    for (int i=0; i<10; i++) {
      print.print(text);
      try { sleep((long)(Math.random() * 100));}
     catch (InterruptedException e) {}
    } // end for
    System.out.println("writer of " +text+" has finished");
  }
}
```

– In the class Printer1, describe the behavior of the print method.

– Describe the behavior of a thread of type Writer2 (explain the run() method).

– Launch the execution of Prog56. Why is the result of the prints illegible?

– Change in the class Printer1 the signature of the print method to public synchronized void print (String t) and restart the execution of Prog56.

– What is the point of the synchronized method?

Exercise 5: program a task with an initial delay and a periodicity

We wish to teach a student the multiplication table for 7, and this is why we want to program a task that displays the multiplication table of 7 every 4 seconds and with an initial delay of 2 seconds. The result is obtained in the following form:

Do you still want to learn the multiplication table? (y/n)

The multiplication table for 7 is:

1 * 7 = 7
2 * 7 = 14
3 * 7 = 21

4 * 7 = 28
5 * 7 = 35
6 * 7 = 42
7 * 7 = 49
8 * 7 = 56
9 * 7 = 63
10 * 7 = 70

PS: Any answer other than "y" cancels the programming.

Exercise 6: shared variables: internal class

Consider the two following classes (the class Parrot20 is called internal class because it is located inside the class MathsParrots20), and there is a single java file called MathsParrots20.java.

```
public class MathsParrots20{
 private int counter;
 public static void main(String args[]) {
  new MathsParrots20();
 }
 public MathsParrots20() {
  counter = 1;
  Parrot20 parrotA = ncw Parrot20("coco", 10);
  Parrot20 parrotB = new Parrot20("hello", 10);
  parrotA.start();
  parrotB.start();
  try {
   parrotA.join();
   parrotB.join();
  }
  catch(InterruptedException e) { }
  System.out.println("counter = "+counter);
 }

 class Parrot20 extends Thread {
  private String cri = null;
```

```
  private int fois = 0;
  public Parrot20(String s, int i)  {
   cry = s;
   times = i;
  }
  public void repeat() {
   String repeat = cry + " " + counter;
   System.out.println(repeat);
   counter++;
   try { Thread.sleep((int)(Math.random()*1000)); }
   catch(InterruptedException e) { }
  }
  public void run(){
   for (int n=0; n<fois; n++)   repeat();
  }
 }
}
```

– Launch and examine the execution.

– *Hint*: join() is used in order to display the value of the counter before the end of the two threads. Due to the visibility rules in Java, the counter variable is visible/accessible from the Parrot20 class and therefore for both parrotA and parrotB threads. The two threads therefore access a shared space common to all variables, unlike the processes that possess their own work space separate from other processes.

– Reuse the simulation of a race to simulate a race between five runners A, B, C, D and E and display the rank of each runner.

Example:

– A has arrived in first place

– B has arrived in second place

– D has arrived in third place

– …

Exercise 7: shared variables: global variable (static)

Before beginning: under Java, each letter can be coded via the char type that also has a whole value. Test and examine the following code:

```
System.out.println('A');
System.out.println('A'+0);
System.out.println('A'+1);
System.out.println((char)('A' + 0));
System.out.println((char)('A' + 1));
System.out.println("Display the alphabet:");
  for (int i = 0; i < 26; i++) {
    System.out.print((char)('A' + i)+" ");
  }
```

– Reuse the example of a race to simulate a race between five runners A, B, C, D and E and display the rank for each runner. You should use a loop to launch the five threads.

Example of execution:

– A has arrived in first place

– B has arrived in second place

– D has arrived in third place

– …

– Simulate the four threads A, B, C and D, which calculate respectively the factorial of 4, 5, 6 and 7. If the order of termination is A, B, C and D, you should also display:

A is very fast
B is fast
C is average
D is slow

Exercise 8: synchronization of threads

This exercise deals with the problems of concurrent access to a bank account (resource-sharing in general). For the following Counter class, its method Nulloperation is meant to leave the level at 0.

```
public class Counter {
  private int balance = 0;
  public void operationNulle(int sum) {
    balance += sum;
    System.out.print(" add " + sum);
   balance -= sum;
    System.out.println(" remove " + sum);
  }
  public int getBalance() {
    return balance;
  }
}
```

Consider the following class that contains the thread Operation and the primary thread:

```
public class Operation extends Thread {
  private Counter Counter;
  public Operation(String nom, Counter Counter) {
         super(name);
    this.Counter = Counter;
  }
  public void run() {
         while (true) {
      int i = (int) (Math.random() * 1001);
      String nom = getName();
      System.out.println(" I am thread:" +name);
      Counter.operationNulle(i);
      int balance = Counter.getBalance();
      if (balance!= 0) {
```

```
 System.out.println(" I am thread " + name + ":**balance=" +
balance);
 System.exit(1);
   }
  }
 }
public static void main(String[] args) {
  Counter Counter = new Counter();
  for (int i = 0; i < 3; i++) {
   Operation operation = new Operation("" + (char)('A' + i),
Counter);
   operation.start();
  }
 }
}
```

Question: examine the code and execute the Operation class.

Determine the encountered problem: operationNull should leave the Counter balance unchanged (at 0), and yet, after a moment, the balance changes from 0. Explain.

Modify the code to prevent this problem.

Exercise 9: applet and thread

An applet is a small Java destined to be downloaded and executed through a web browser. Once compiled, an applet must be called in an html file. Then, in order to be executed, the html file will be visualized in a browser or in the appletviewer tool.

Copy the following code into a file named Prog11.java.

```
import java.awt.Graphics ;
import java.applet.Applet;
public class Prog11 extends Applet {
```

```
  public void paint (Graphics g) {
    g.drawLine (10, 30, 200, 30);
    g.drawRect (20, 40, 100, 50);
    g.drawOval (140, 40, 50, 50);
    g.drawString ("hello!", 10, 120);
  }
}
```

Our class inherits the Applet class: simply redefine the paint method using the draw method of the Graphics class.

Copy the following code into a file titled drawing.html

```
<html> <body>    <applet code="Prog11.class" width=350 height=150>
</applet> </body></html>
```

Execute drawing.html (by clicking directly on the file), or the command-line using appletviewer drawing.html. You can also execute Prog11.java under Netbeans. For the browser, just make sure the java plugin is present.

Explain the different methods in paint.

Consider the following class:

```
import java.awt.Graphics;
import java.awt.Color;
import java.applet.Applet;
public class Prog12 extends Applet {
  public void init( ) {
    setSize(220,120);
    setForeground(Color.red);
    setBackground(Color.white); }
  public void paint(Graphics g) {
    g.drawLine(10, 30, 200, 30);
    g.fillRect(20, 40, 100, 50);
    g.setColor(Color.blue);
    g.drawOval(140, 40, 50, 50);
```

```
  g.drawString("text draw", 10, 60);
}
}
```

The init method is called only once at the creation of the applet.

Initialization of the applet: modification of its size, and the background and drawing colors.

Execute the applet.

Explain the different methods in init and paint.

Consider the following CounterThread class:

```
public class CounterThread extends Applet implements Runnable {
 Thread t;
 int Count;
 public void init()  {
  Count=0;
  t=new Thread(this); // t must take an object as a parameter
  t.start();
 }
 public void run() {
  while (Count < 20)  {
   Count++;
   repaint();
   try {Thread.sleep(1000);   } catch (InterruptedException e) {}
  }
 }
 public void paint(Graphics g) {
  g.drawString(Integer.toString(Count),10,10);
  System.out.println("Count= "+Count);
 }
}
```

Execute the applet and examine the result.

Would it be possible to declare the CounterThread class differently, why?

I can pass this to the Thread builder, why?

Modify the previous code for Counter ten times faster and without stopping.

Exercise 10: concurrent access with semaphores

Consider the following class:

```
import java.util.concurrent.Semaphore;
 class Process2 extends Thread{
   private int id;
   private Semaphore sem;
   public Process2(int i, Semaphore s)  {
      id = i;
      sem = s;}
   private void busy()
   {
      try{sleep((int)(Math.random()*1000));}
                   catch (InterruptedException e){}
   }
   private void noncritical()   {
      System.out.println("Thread " + id + "is not in the critical section");
      busy();
   }
   private void critical()   {
      System.out.println("Thread " + id + "enters the critical section");
      busy();
      System.out.println("Thread " + id + "exits the critical section");
   }
   public void run()   {
         noncritical();
```

```
        try {
            sem.acquire();
        } catch (InterruptedException e){ }
        critical();
        sem.release();
    }
    public static void main(String[] args)    {
Semaphore sem = new Semaphore(4);
       Process2[] p = new Process2[4];
       for (int i = 0; i < 4; i++)       {
          p[i] = new Process2(i, sem);
          p[i].start();
       }
    }
}
```

Questions:

1) Launch the execution and explain the Semaphore declaration sem – new Semaphore(4); that is, the point of the number 4, what does 4 mean here?

2) Restart the execution by changing the number 4 to 3, 2, 1 and 0, respectively. Explain for each one.

3) With the Semaphore declaration, sem = new Semaphore(1); put sem.release(); in comment. Execute and explain.

Exercise 11: Sleeping barber's problem (producer/consumer with semaphore)

A barber owns a salon with one barber seat and a waiting room containing N waiting seats.

– If he has no customers, the barber sits on the barber seat.

– When a customer arrives:

- If the waiting room is full, the customer comes back later.

- If the barber is asleep, he wakes him up, sits on the barber seat and waits for his haircut.

- If the barber is busy when the customer arrives, the customer sits and falls asleep on one of the N chairs in the waiting room, he must wait for the barber seat to be available.

– When the barber is done with one haircut, he exits the customer and goes to wake up one of the customers in the waiting room.

– If the waiting room is empty, the barber goes back to sleep on his barber seat and waits for another customer to arrive.

The point of this exercise is to associate a thread with the barber as well as with every customer and program a sleeping barber session in Java. The use of semaphores is required to guarantee the mutual exclusion among the threads.

Hint: A client is characterized by its name and three semaphores: FreeChairs, Wake, BarberChair.

FreeChairs: manages the mutual exclusion in relation to the waiting room.

Wake: use in order to allow the client to wake the barber if the latter is asleep.

BarberChair: manages the mutual exclusion in relation to the barber chair.

A barber is characterized by two semaphores Wake, BarberChair.

Upon initialization, ensure that the two semaphores – Wake, BarberChair – are in common with barber and the client threads.

Example of initialization:

Barber c = new Barber(Wake, BarberChair);

Client cl = new Client("Client " + i + ":", FreeChairs, Wake, BarberChair);

In the Semaphore class, the tryAcquire() method attempts to acquire a chip to access the critical section (returns true in case of success, false in case of failure).

Example: while (!FreeChairs.tryAcquire()) sleep(5000); could be used in the client's run in order to put itself into wait-mode if there are no free chairs.

Exercise 12: entry/exit management of a parking lot

In this Exercise, we wish to count the entries and exits of the vehicles in a parking lot to display the number of available spaces in the parking lot every time a car exits. The parking lot's operation is simple: there is one single entry to the parking lot that has a capacity of N.

The point of this exercise is to count the number of free spaces in the parking lot using only one shared variable.

This variable must be declared in a class Car (the thread which represents the behavior of a Car) as follows: static int cont=N;

One single class is necessary in this exercise (Car class), and the latter is characterized by an *integer number* i and a *semaphore s*.

Exercise 13: philosophers' dinner

This problem is a great classic [DIJ 70]. Five philosophers are reunited to perform two major activities: think and eat. Each philosopher thinks for a random amount of time, eats (if possible) during a random amount of time, then goes back to thinking. When a philosopher asks to eat, a plate of spaghetti is waiting. The five plates are laid out around a round table as shown in the figure below:

For a philosopher to eat his spaghetti, two forks are necessary: his (the one on the right) and his neighbor's to the left. Naturally, if one of the neighbors is already eating, the philosopher cannot eat and must wait for one or both of the forks to free up.

The solution to this problem must be as optimized as possible: one philosopher wanting but not being able to eat must wait his turn without using up CPU time uselessly.

Each philosopher performs the cycle a number of times: THINK, ASK FOR FOOD, EAT.

We naturally cannot see two philosophers eating side-by-side at the same time.

One thread can see itself be denied access to a resource during an undetermined amount of time. It is then said that the thread is starving. A philosopher cannot eat during a set amount of time when starving. However, there is a situation of inter-blocking when all philosophers attempt to take a fork at the same time.

– Program a solution in java that uses two classes: *Dinner* (contains the "main", etc.) and *Philo* (thread corresponding to the activity of a philosopher).

Example of execution:

Philo0 is thinking
Philo2 is thinking
Philo1 is thinking
Philo3 is thinking
Philo4 is thinking
Philo4 wants to eat
Philo4 is eating
Philo0 wants to eat
Philo3 wants to eat
Philo1 wants to eat
Philo1 is eating
Philo2 wants to eat

Philo4 has finished eating
Philo3 is eating
Philo4 is thinking
Philo1 has finished eating
Philo1 is thinking
Philo0 is eating
Philo4 wants to eat
Philo1 wants to eat
Philo3 has finished eating
Philo3 is thinking
Philo2 is eating
Philo0 has finished eating
Philo0 is thinking
Philo4 is eating
...

– During your tests, ensure that no two side-by-side philosophers are eating at the same time, and that there is no starvation, and of course, that there is no inter-blocking.

Exercise 14: producer/consumer

Consider the three following java classes: B.java, Producer.java and Consumer.java.

The Producer and the Consumer share an object b of type B.

```
class B {
private Object [ ] buffer;
private int taille ;
private int prem, der, nbObj;
public B (int t) {
taille = t;
buffer = new Object [taille];
prem = 0;
der = 0;
nbObj = 0;
}
```

```
public synchronized void depose (Object obj) {
while (cond1) try {wait ();}catch ( InterruptedException e) {}
buffer [der] = obj;
der = (der + 1) % size;
nbObj = nbObj + 1;
notify ();
}
public synchronized Object collected () {
while (cond2) try {wait ();}catch ( InterruptedException e) {}
Object obj = buffer [prem];
buffer [prem] = null;
prem = (prem + 1) % size;
nbObj = nbObj - 1;
notify ();
return (obj);
}
} // end B

class Producer implements Runnable {
private B b;
private int val;
public Producer (B b) {this.b = b;}
public void run () {
while (true) {
b.putsdown (new Integer (val));
System.out.println (Thread.currentThread ().getName () +"has put down" +
val);
val ++;
try {Thread.sleep ((int)( Math.random ()*100));}catch ( Interrupted
Exception e) {}
}
}// end run
}// endProducer
```

```
class Consumer implements Runnable {
private B b;
public Consumer (B b) {this.b = b;}
public void run () {
Integer val;
while (true) {
val = (Integer) b.preleve();
System.out.println ( Thread.currentThread ().getName () +"collected" + val );
try {Thread.sleep ((int)( Math.random ()*300));}catch ( Interrupted
Exception e) {}
}
}// end run
}// end Consumer
```

– Complete the code of class B by giving cond1 and cond2.

– In the putsdown method, what is the role of the instruction der = (der + 1) % size?

– Based on the previous question, what is thc type of buffer used for an object of type B?

– Write the class Primary.java, the latter launches two threads P of type Producer and C of type Consumer. The name of the thread P must be Prod and the namc of the thread C must be Consu. The sizc of the shared buffer is 4.

Exercise 15: thread synchronization

You are responsible for a large computer project tasked with piloting automatic cars. Unfortunately, they do not drive in the same direction and the road that these cars use has a one-way section. At any moment, more than one car (N in the general case) can circulate on the one-way road on condition that they are going the same way, if at least one car is present on the one-way segment, the cars on the other side will have to wait for the road to be available.

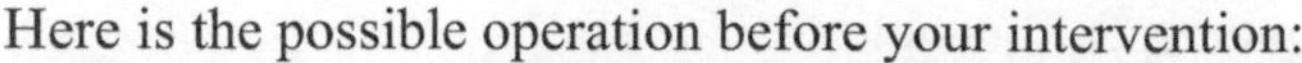

Here is the possible operation before your intervention:

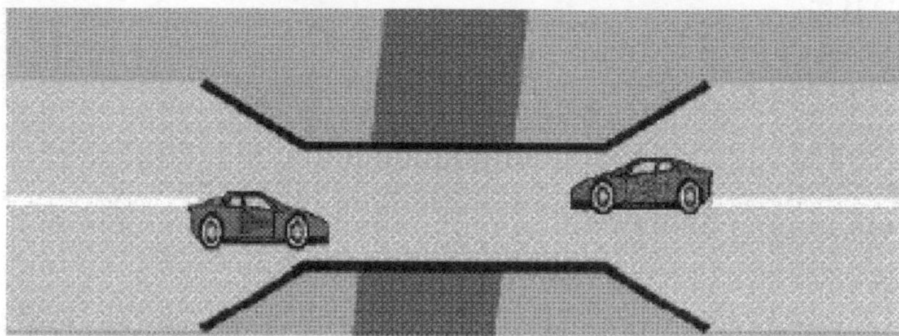

Use thread synchronization to sort this problem.

Exercise 16: factorial and Fibonacci with the TCP sockets

Consider the following function:

Function factorial (n: int): integer
Beginning
  If n > 1
    Return n * factorial(n - 1)
  Else
    Return 1
  End if
End

– Implement this function on the server side and create a client/server model using TCP sockets under Java; the client will have an integer n (>=0) to the client, and the latter must respond with a factorial (n).

– The Fibonacci sequence is a series of integers in which each entry is the sum of the two integers that preceded it. It generally begins with the numbers 0 and 1 (sometimes 1 and 1) and its first numbers are: 0, 1, 1, 2, 3, 5, 8, 13, 21, etc. Your client must now send an integer n to the server, and the latter must respond with the nth number of the Fibonacci sequence. For example, if the client sends 8 to the server, it recovers 13 (the eighth number).

Exercise 17: mystery with the TCP sockets

– What is the mystery method of the following Java class?

```
//// A.java
import java.io.*;
public class A{
   public static void mystery (InputStream in, OutputStream out) throws
IOException {
        byte buf[ ] = new byte[1024]; int n;
           while((n=in.read(buf))!=-1)  out.write(buf,0,n);
         in.close();
         out.close();
  }
}
```

– Consider the following two java classes:

```
////////// Client.java
import java.io.*;
import java.net.*;
public class Client{
   public static void main(String []args) throws IOException     {
      Socket sock = new Socket(InetAddress.getLocalHost(),9001);
      A.mystery(new
              FileInputStream("./src/test1"),sock.getOutputStream());
      sock.close();
   }
}
```

```
//// Server.java
import java.io.*;
import java.net.*;
```

```
public class Serveur{
   public static void main(String []args) throws IOException {
      Socket sock = new ServerSocket(9001).accept();
      A.mystery(sock.getInputStream(),new
              FileOutputStream("./src/test2"));
      sock.close();
   }
}
```

– What does this application do by executing the two classes (Client and Server) in localhost?

– By using two different machines (a machine on the client side and another on the server side), what will be the objective of this application?

Exercise 18: managing a counter with the TCP sockets

We have a list of bank counters. A counter is characterized by its *account holder*, its *number* and its *balance*.

The client connects to the server and sends an integer **M,** the server must respond with the list of counter account holders who have a higher balance than **M.**

– Write the two classes ClientCounter and ServeurCounter according to the TCP sockets model in java.

– Now, your client must connect to the server by sending a counter number in order to recover all information on this counter (under the form of an object for a first version and the form of a chain of characters for a second version). Make the necessary modifications to your code in order to answer this question.

Exercise 19: applet and TCP sockets

Create the following client/server model:

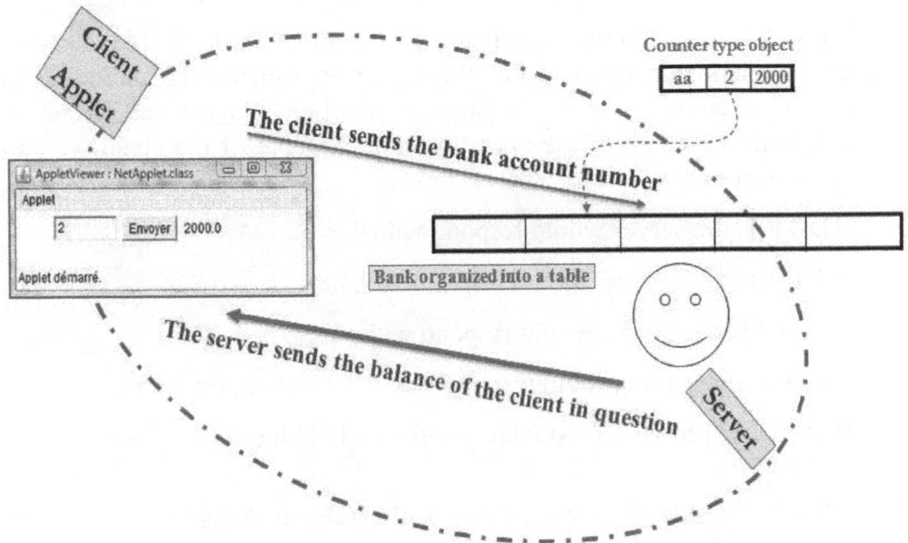

For a color version of the figure, see www.iste.co.uk/benmammar/java.zip

Improve the HMI on the client side and the processing on the server side in order to perform classic banking operations:

– Open a new Counter;

– Add money to a Counter with a known number;

– Withdraw from a Counter with a known number;

– Display the name of the account holder and the balance of a Counter with a known number;

– Display the Counter number when the name of the account holder is known;

– Display the average sum of the balances of all the Counters;

– Display the Counter list.

Exercise 20: arithmetic operations with TCP sockets

In this exercise, ADD, MUL, DIV and SUB correspond, respectively, to operations of adding, multiplying, dividing and subtracting.

Your objective is to create a client/server application using TCP sockets. The client sends two operands to the server as well as the operation to perform (all three in the form of a single chain of characters), and the server responds with the result of the operation. For example, if the client were to send to the server:

– ADD 6 1, the server would respond with 7.

– MUL 10 88, the latter would respond with 880.

– SOUS 5 9, the server would respond with -4.

– DIV 9 8, the server would respond with 1.125. (Real division).

– PARIS 6 7, the server would respond with hhhhh error.

Exercise 21: multiplication tables with TCP sockets

– Create a client/server model using TCP sockets java; the client sends an integer to the server (4 for example), and the latter responds with the multiplication table of the integer.

The client would, for example, have to display:

Multiplication table of 4:

0 4 8 12 16 20 24 28 32 36 40

– Your client must now send a table of integers, saying {1, 6, 8, 9, 13, 10}.

– The server must respond with the sub-table containing only even integers ({6, 8, 10}).

Exercise 22: low-level manipulations of TCP sockets

Using low-level TCP socket manipulations (write of OutputStream and read InputStream), write a client/server model in which the client sends the server a phrase containing two words (ex. PARIS MADRID).

The server will spread via the same sentence but over two lines (each word on one line).

In this example, the server will respond with:

PARIS
MADRID

Exercise 23: manipulating character chains with RMI

– Using Java RMI, write a remote method to calculate the inverse of a word. For this, we need to write the shared interface between the client and the server, the client implementation and the server implementation.

– Add a second remote method to return the sub-string containing the four characters at the beginning of this word.

– Add a third remote method to find out whether the word is a palindrome.

Exercise 24: Fibonacci with RMI

The Fibonacci sequence is a series of integers in which each number is the sum of the two numbers before it. It generally begins with 1 and its first numbers are: 1, 1, 2, 3, 5, 8, 13, 21, etc.

Using Java RMI, write a remote method that has a parameter of number *n* and that returns the *n* first integers of the sequence. Sending 5, for example, to the server, the latter will respond with the following chain of characters: 1, 1, 2, 3, 5.

Exercise 25: bowtie with RMI

Using Java RMI, write a remote method that receives a chain of characters with an odd number of characters (you will have to perform a test on the length of the word) and displays it in the shape of a bowtie. For example:

```
h   o
he lo
```

hello
he lo
h o

Exercise 26: registry service with RMI

We wish to implement a registry service that records names and phone numbers and allows the user to access them using a name. The registry must be accessible remotely via RMI. We consider that the name and number are chains of characters.

– Define an RMI interface that responds to these specifications.

– Develop a server object implanting this interface.

– Develop a client that questions the aforementioned server object.

Bibliography

[AIC 17] AICAS, available at: http://www.aicas.com/, 2017.

[DIJ 71] DIJKSTRA E.W., "Hierarchical ordering of sequential processes" in BRINCH HANSEN P. (ed.), *The Origin of Concurrent Programming*, Springer, New York, 1971.

[ORA 17a] ORACLE, "Class Thread", available at: https://docs.oracle.com/javase/7/docs/api/java/lang/Thread.html, 2017.

[ORA 17b] ORACLE, "Class ThreadGroup" available at: https://docs.oracle.com/javase/7/docs/api/java/lang/ThreadGroup.html, 2017.

[JAV 17a] JAVA® COMMUNITY PROCESS, "Real-Time Specification for Java", available at: http://www.rtsj.org/, 2017.

[JAV 17b] JAVA® COMMUNITY PROCESS, "Package javax.realtime", available at: http://www.rtsj.org/specjavadoc/javax/realtime/package-summary.html, 2017.

[STA 88] STANKOVIC J.A., "Misconceptions about real-time computing: a serious problem for next-generation systems", *Computer*, vol.21, no.10, pp.10–19, 1988.

[TAN 01] TANENBAUM A.S., "Multimedia Operating Systems" in *Modern Operating Systems*, 2nd ed., Prentice-Hall, Upper Saddle River, 2001.

[TIM 17] TIMESYS, available at: http://www.timesys.com/, 2017.

[UCI 17] UNIVERSITY OF CALIFORNIA, "Irvine", available at: http://www.uci.edu/, 2017.

Index

A, C, D

G, H, I

J, K, L

M, N, O

Q, R, S

T, V, W

Other titles from

in

Computer Engineering

2017

HÉLIODORE Frédéric, NAKIB Amir, ISMAIL Boussaad, OUCHRAA Salma, SCHMITT Laurent
Metaheuristics for Intelligent Electrical Networks
(Metaheuristics Set – Volume 10)

MA Haiping, SIMON Dan
Evolutionary Computation with Biogeography-based Optimization
(Metaheuristics Set – Volume 8)

PÉTROWSKI Alain, BEN-HAMIDA Sana
Evolutionary Algorithms
(Metaheuristics Set – Volume 9)

2016

BLUM Christian, FESTA Paola
Metaheuristics for String Problems in Bio-informatics
(Metaheuristics Set – Volume 6)

DEROUSSI Laurent
Metaheuristics for Logistics
(Metaheuristics Set – Volume 4)

DHAENENS Clarisse and JOURDAN Laetitia
Metaheuristics for Big Data
(Metaheuristics Set – Volume 5)

LABADIE Nacima, PRINS Christian, PRODHON Caroline
Metaheuristics for Vehicle Routing Problems
(Metaheuristics Set – Volume 3)

LEROY Laure
Eyestrain Reduction in Stereoscopy

LUTTON Evelyne, PERROT Nathalie, TONDA Albert
Evolutionary Algorithms for Food Science and Technology
(Metaheuristics Set – Volume 7)

MAGOULÈS Frédéric, ZHAO Hai-Xiang
Data Mining and Machine Learning in Building Energy Analysis

RIGO Michel
Advanced Graph Theory and Combinatorics

2015

BARBIER Franck, RECOUSSINE Jean-Luc
COBOL Software Modernization: From Principles to Implementation with the BLU AGE® Method

CHEN Ken
Performance Evaluation by Simulation and Analysis with Applications to Computer Networks

CLERC Maurice
Guided Randomness in Optimization
(Metaheuristics Set – Volume 1)

DURAND Nicolas, GIANAZZA David, GOTTELAND Jean-Baptiste, ALLIOT Jean-Marc
Metaheuristics for Air Traffic Management
(Metaheuristics Set – Volume 2)

MAGOULÈS Frédéric, ROUX François-Xavier, HOUZEAUX Guillaume
Parallel Scientific Computing

MUNEESAWANG Paisarn, YAMMEN Suchart
Visual Inspection Technology in the Hard Disk Drive Industry

2014

BOULANGER Jean-Louis
Formal Methods Applied to Industrial Complex Systems

BOULANGER Jean-Louis
Formal Methods Applied to Complex Systems: Implementation of the B Method

GARDI Frédéric, BENOIST Thierry, DARLAY Julien, ESTELLON Bertrand, MEGEL Romain
Mathematical Programming Solver based on Local Search

KRICHEN Saoussen, CHAOUACHI Jouhaina
Graph-related Optimization and Decision Support Systems

LARRIEU Nicolas, VARET Antoine
Rapid Prototyping of Software for Avionics Systems: Model-oriented Approaches for Complex Systems Certification

OUSSALAH Mourad Chabane
Software Architecture 1
Software Architecture 2

PASCHOS Vangelis Th
Combinatorial Optimization – 3-volume series, 2nd Edition
Concepts of Combinatorial Optimization – Volume 1, 2nd Edition
Problems and New Approaches – Volume 2, 2nd Edition
Applications of Combinatorial Optimization – Volume 3, 2nd Edition

QUESNEL Flavien
Scheduling of Large-scale Virtualized Infrastructures: Toward Cooperative Management

RIGO Michel
Formal Languages, Automata and Numeration Systems 1: Introduction to Combinatorics on Words
Formal Languages, Automata and Numeration Systems 2: Applications to Recognizability and Decidability

SAINT-DIZIER Patrick
Musical Rhetoric: Foundations and Annotation Schemes

TOUATI Sid, DE DINECHIN Benoit
Advanced Backend Optimization

2013

ANDRÉ Etienne, SOULAT Romain
The Inverse Method: Parametric Verification of Real-time Embedded Systems

BOULANGER Jean-Louis
Safety Management for Software-based Equipment

DELAHAYE Daniel, PUECHMOREL Stéphane
Modeling and Optimization of Air Traffic

FRANCOPOULO Gil
LMF — Lexical Markup Framework

GHÉDIRA Khaled
Constraint Satisfaction Problems

ROCHANGE Christine, UHRIG Sascha, SAINRAT Pascal
Time-Predictable Architectures

WAHBI Mohamed
Algorithms and Ordering Heuristics for Distributed Constraint Satisfaction Problems

ZELM Martin *et al.*
Enterprise Interoperability

2012

ARBOLEDA Hugo, ROYER Jean-Claude
Model-Driven and Software Product Line Engineering

BLANCHET Gérard, DUPOUY Bertrand
Computer Architecture

BOULANGER Jean-Louis
Industrial Use of Formal Methods: Formal Verification

BOULANGER Jean-Louis
Formal Method: Industrial Use from Model to the Code

CALVARY Gaëlle, DELOT Thierry, SÈDES Florence, TIGLI Jean-Yves
Computer Science and Ambient Intelligence

MAHOUT Vincent
Assembly Language Programming: ARM Cortex-M3 2.0: Organization, Innovation and Territory

MARLET Renaud
Program Specialization

SOTO Maria, SEVAUX Marc, ROSSI André, LAURENT Johann
Memory Allocation Problems in Embedded Systems: Optimization Methods

2011

BICHOT Charles-Edmond, SIARRY Patrick
Graph Partitioning

BOULANGER Jean-Louis
Static Analysis of Software: The Abstract Interpretation

CAFERRA Ricardo
Logic for Computer Science and Artificial Intelligence

HOMES Bernard
Fundamentals of Software Testing

KORDON Fabrice, HADDAD Serge, PAUTET Laurent, PETRUCCI Laure
Distributed Systems: Design and Algorithms

KORDON Fabrice, HADDAD Serge, PAUTET Laurent, PETRUCCI Laure
Models and Analysis in Distributed Systems

LORCA Xavier
Tree-based Graph Partitioning Constraint

TRUCHET Charlotte, ASSAYAG Gerard
Constraint Programming in Music

VICAT-BLANC PRIMET Pascale *et al.*
Computing Networks: From Cluster to Cloud Computing

2010

AUDIBERT Pierre
Mathematics for Informatics and Computer Science

BABAU Jean-Philippe *et al.*
Model Driven Engineering for Distributed Real-Time Embedded Systems 2009

BOULANGER Jean-Louis
Safety of Computer Architectures

MONMARCHE Nicolas *et al.*
Artificial Ants

PANETTO Hervé, BOUDJLIDA Nacer
Interoperability for Enterprise Software and Applications 2010

SIGAUD Olivier *et al.*
Markov Decision Processes in Artificial Intelligence

SOLNON Christine
Ant Colony Optimization and Constraint Programming

AUBRUN Christophe, SIMON Daniel, SONG Ye-Qiong *et al.*
Co-design Approaches for Dependable Networked Control Systems

2009

FOURNIER Jean-Claude
Graph Theory and Applications

GUEDON Jeanpierre
The Mojette Transform / Theory and Applications

JARD Claude, ROUX Olivier
Communicating Embedded Systems / Software and Design

LECOUTRE Christophe
Constraint Networks / Targeting Simplicity for Techniques and Algorithms

2008

BANÂTRE Michel, MARRÓN Pedro José, OLLERO Hannibal, WOLITZ Adam
Cooperating Embedded Systems and Wireless Sensor Networks

MERZ Stephan, NAVET Nicolas
Modeling and Verification of Real-time Systems

PASCHOS Vangelis Th
Combinatorial Optimization and Theoretical Computer Science: Interfaces and Perspectives

WALDNER Jean-Baptiste
Nanocomputers and Swarm Intelligence

2007

BENHAMOU Frédéric, JUSSIEN Narendra, O'SULLIVAN Barry
Trends in Constraint Programming

JUSSIEN Narendra
A to Z of Sudoku

2006

BABAU Jean-Philippe *et al.*
From MDD Concepts to Experiments and Illustrations – DRES 2006

HABRIAS Henri, FRAPPIER Marc
Software Specification Methods

MURAT Cecile, PASCHOS Vangelis Th
Probabilistic Combinatorial Optimization on Graphs

PANETTO Hervé, BOUDJLIDA Nacer
Interoperability for Enterprise Software and Applications 2006 / IFAC-IFIP I-ESA'2006

2005

GÉRARD Sébastien *et al.*
Model Driven Engineering for Distributed Real Time Embedded Systems

PANETTO Hervé
Interoperability of Enterprise Software and Applications 2005